THE NEW TRINITY

THE
NEW TRINITY

Your Secular Pathway
to Personal Spirituality

JACK BURCH

DeVorss Publications
Camarillo, California

ISBN: 9780875168616
FIRST EDITION, 2011

DeVorss & Company, Publisher
PO Box 1389
Camarillo CA 93011-1389
www.devorss.com

Printed in the United States of America

Library of Congress Cataloging-in-Publication Data

Burch, Jack J., 1936-
  The new trinity : your secular pathway to personal spirituality
/ by Jack J. Burch. -- 1st ed.
      p. cm.
  Includes bibliographical references.
  ISBN 978-0-87516-861-6 (pbk. : alk. paper) 1. Spirituality. I.
Title.
  BL624.B865 2010
  191--dc22
                                        2010041130

TABLE OF CONTENTS

LIST OF ILLUSTRATIONS / TABLES

PREFACE

The very process of beginning this Preface—considering various positions, then proceeding to one—illustrates the marvelous capability we, as humans, have in discriminating among our choices and exercising our free will in co-creating our universe. Yet, the simple statement of this capability raises many questions as to how this common activity of co-creativity becomes manifest, and how we are to best proceed with responsibility and integrity in using this capacity for the peace and happiness of our self and others. Such are the questions that I've attempted to answer in *The New Trinity*.

The Pathway, in the subtitle, refers to the several topics covered in providing a total philosophical perspective. The resulting personal practice incorporates a synthesis of archetypal mythology, metaphysical philosophy, a personal psychology, and mindfulness—all combining to define the spiritual identity of each individual.

This book evolved over a number of years as I sought to determine a comprehensive spiritual philosophy sufficient to satisfy my own level of understanding, but also suitable for instructing others. It has been my lifelong nature to be an explorer of things beyond the apparent, from engineering useful devices from scientific principles in my first career, exploring of caves and mountains as an avocation, engaging in new entrepreneurial business models, and finally to researching and formulating a metaphysical philosophy for conscious beings. A long-term goal, fundamental to developing this book, was to determine a new model linking thoughts, judgments, and emotions. Following progressive iterations over a number of years, i.e., following a succession of approximations that built upon the preceding one, this model evolved into the form presented in a geometric format and supported by textual elaboration.

As a young scientist, one of my supervisors once questioned, "Why can't we be researching the relationship of human life to the powers of the universe, rather than developing military systems?" The idea intrigued me through the years until I began to undertake the quest. The teachings and teachers of Religious Science reoriented me toward spirituality from my semi-agnostic position, and I served with them as a practitioner for five years. Early training in a research laboratory dictated that I take a systems approach requiring extensive research from many related disciplines encountered along the pathway. And yet, echoing from my student years, the writings of existentialist Jean Paul Sartre, though an atheist, provided a continuing influence emphasizing the primacy of free will and personal responsibility.

A *natural* philosophy of spirituality, *secular* through an absence of the "transcendent supreme being" common to many religions, does not remove the inherent divine-like nature of freedom and goodness with an unlimited potential for peace, compassion, love, and joy, and the seemingly magical occurrences of serendipity. The progressively creative agency of consciousness—providing life's meaning and value, and allowing for humanistic concerns—precludes its assignment to reductionism and the materialism of physics so prevalent in scientific theories. The leading hypothesis here is that conscious life exists in parallel with the physical universe, yet is reflected within it. With the limits of human knowledge, science cannot at this time, and may never, provide all the answers regarding the linkage between individual consciousness and its experiences and manifestations, including brain activity. Here the term *Generative Principle* is introduced as this intermediary, which together with consciousness and its manifested experiences, constitute the *New Trinity*. The question will arise, "Isn't God this linkage?" Though the answer may be "yes," the Generative Principle certainly cannot be equated with the God of traditional religion. Human consciousness alone is sufficient for spirituality, requiring neither a transcendental being nor religion.

The preparation of this book was assisted by conversations with numerous acquaintances and instructors along the pathway, and my gratitude is extended to all. I would particularly like to thank Dr. Catherine Monserrat who provided a critical reading and numerous suggestions especially in the field of psychology, and Stephanie Sorensen for her insightful editing. And an appreciation with *anam cara* is extended to the reader who suggested *New Trinity* as title, the late Joan Vanderhor. I am especially thankful for my wife Lynda's patience, understanding, and encouragement during the years of preparation.

INTRODUCTION

You can change your life experiences by way of thought, but the secret is to know, understand, and speak from the nature of your own being. The reality of your existence is not what it seems to be because you are actually a spiritual being living in what appears as the ever-changing material world. This true spiritual identity is much more than the physical body that you inhabit. In this book, you will discover a new self-identity independent of, and unrestricted by, past history. You will start afresh and continue to do so each moment.

The universe does directly respond to your thoughts in producing your experiences, so it is important to learn the inner dialog that produces the peace and joy that you desire. Your experiences are the product of your thinking, but there is an intermediary in-between serving as the source of the world you inhabit. Here, we identify a divine New Trinity formed by (1) the conscious you, (2) the generative source of all things, and (3) your experiential world. You are an all-important component in this Trinity because the source cannot do it without you. Rather, it works *with* you and *through* you. You are not a casual attendant in this worldly procession, nor are you a victim. You are an initiating force. Therefore, it is necessary for you to learn to be in charge of your experiences.

You will discover a new spiritual identity for yourself in this book. Spirituality is an important need for all people, yet many limit their spiritual experience to the traditional religions of their culture. In most Western religions, for instance, an external deity is assumed to be the primary provider of daily experiences, resulting in the typical resignation: "It is God's will." In contrast, the philosophy in this book reveals that *you* are in charge and have the means to change your life. Yes, there is a source that you may consider as divine, but one that is responsive to your thinking without the judgmental characteristics generally assigned to the male God of traditional religions. The source within the New Trinity is intimately receptive to you without judgment.

The myth of the judgmental, male God was common to earlier Mid-Eastern cultures before it was adopted by Semitic cultures in the Bible. Yet there are other myths, even older, upon which to base divinity. The term "myth" as used here does not imply a fictional construction, but rather is a means for representing complex ideas in approachable terms, akin to metaphor and allegory. Lasting myths would not endure if they did not resonate with archetypical content in the subconscious mind. There is no empirical evidence establishing the absolute truth for any myth or religion, yet each provides a means of understanding, especially if supported by comprehensive and systematic thought. The myth of the judgmental, male God that has led Western culture to this point has served important functions. But now it is time to explore a new concept of divinity that better serves the individual and humanity.

The most enduring myth of all time is that of the Goddess. Whereas the concept of a male God has been dominant for the past few thousand years, the Goddess was intuitively accepted as the principle deity and source of manifestations for at least the prior forty thousand years. The mythical Goddess is an early psychic representation for the archetype of the creative source of the universe. This archetype has been reinterpreted in this book and termed the *Generative Principle*, postulated for the creative process continually operating in our experience.

Here, we explore a spirituality based upon the Generative Principle that incorporates very familiar concepts from psychology including the conscious and subconscious mind. This new interpretation is expanded to describe a higher power that is receptive and responsive, immanent rather than transcendent, comfortable to rely upon, and *requires no intermediary or external religious authority*—providing us with a new myth upon which to base a spiritual philosophy of life.

The Generative Principle responds to each individual consciousness through *natural*, rather than supernatural, processes
employing the creative forces of the universe. In deference to the
generative powers and intelligence involved in forming the physical
world and our experiences, we commonly refer to the Generative
Principle in the pantheistic expression of *Mother Nature*. We observe
interactions between consciousness and resulting experiences with
measurable changes occurring in the brain (Siegel, 2007).
Consciousness and these observable effects have reciprocal influence over one another, and although we do not totally comprehend
the process and mechanism involved, it is not unscientific to give it
a name pending better understanding. We select the Generative
Principle. The Generative Principle, as described here, is analogous
to the scientist's *black box*, wherein the contents are unknown but
the operations and relationships are identified.

Throughout history, science has evolved through a number of
concepts that today seem archaic, such as a flat earth or the earth
being the center of the universe. It has advanced through developments in classical laws of motion, relativity, and quantum mechanics.
Yet, the primary myths of Western society have changed little. It is
reasonable to expect that evolutionary progress is also possible in
fields of religion and philosophy, though there is considerable inertia
in considering new ideas due to intolerance and dogmatic adherence
to traditional concepts of truth. A new myth can lead us into greater
respect for others and mutual cooperation.

There is considerable comfort to be realized through a personal and intimate relationship with the immanent, creative
source, even if you prefer equating Her with the individual or
collective Soul. Establishing that the generative forces of the
universe relate to feminine archetype (as we will do) is useful,
but *alone* is not sufficient for our purposes. One also needs a
personal spiritual practice incorporating individual consciousness in the creative process of this New Trinity. The primary

purpose of this book is to establish a relationship between each individual, the Generative Principle, and experience.

Beyond improving our personal experiences, our relationship with this immanent deity structures the way we view life in the world and influences the organization of society. A new spirituality involving ideas such as mutual acceptance, freedom, and individual worth—with an interpersonal linkage of love—can permeate governing bodies through moral codes and education. Considering the current world turmoil resulting from autocratic, domineering attitudes with intolerance towards individuals and other nations, we would do well to find a new model upon which to base our society.

You, along with others, may wish to change the world in specific ways but, ironically, the pathway to beneficial change is not so much about the *future* as it is a way of being in the *present*. If the future world is to be transformed into a more peaceful and joyful place, the process will begin with "present-moment" changes within individuals like you. Religions that place emphasis upon another world, such as heaven or hell, detract from the immediate task of living and working cooperatively in the here and now.

As you will see, the mechanism of all material change is through the Generative Principle. However, most religions, philosophies, and current psychological disciplines tend to avoid postulating about such a principle: What is its relationship to us? How does it operate? What is its purpose? How can we communicate with it? And, why should we? Whenever things are not directly observable, measurable or predictable, they are considered to lie outside the scientific realm and beyond direct inquiry. In spite of the intangible nature of the Generative Principle, an experiential encounter is not only possible, but also unavoidable, for such an engagement is intrinsic to life in this world.

This book is about developing *intimacy* between your everyday conscious mind and the Generative Principle because togeth-

er you form a most creative team. Your consciousness is more
capable and less limited than you have been taught. While exploring the vast dimensions of your consciousness, you will renew
your spiritual self-identity and find fresh grounding for self-
esteem. You do not have to originate this spiritual nature. It has
always existed but, most often, unrecognized. Your spirituality is
a very personal matter and is not dependent upon your being
religious. You are, as Wayne Dyer has suggested, *a spiritual being
having a human experience*.

Your Spiritual Self, as an aspect of your conscious mind, is composed of favorable attributes such as inherent goodness and freedom,
inner tranquility, uninhibited joy, and unqualified love. These are the
qualities we often deny within ourselves and project onto heroes and
Gods. By finding and embracing this new identity and affirming this
truth in your communion with the Generative Principle, you will
find these attributes reflected in your own experience. An intimate
relationship with Her constitutes your *new personal spirituality*, dis-
solving concepts of guilt and sin.

You communicate with the Generative Principle by thoughts,
emotions, and convictions about who you are, and by your judgments of life's events and their relationship to you. She responds by
offering experiences that seem to say: *Yes, my dear, and so it shall be*.
By examining the structure of thought and emotion, you can gain
insight into the meaning of Her messages and chart a course toward
a more satisfying life.

Because each person's circumstances are unique, no single
treatment of human consciousness can provide the final answers
for everyone. Yet, it is important to have some concept of the
process of *life itself* as a criterion for personal decision and action.
Then, we may meaningfully encounter ourselves and pose the
question: *Is my action—mental or physical—consistent with my reference beliefs?* In other words: *Does this experience reflect the nature of*

my true being? This exploration provides an honest basis for a decision to continue or change our actions. Each of us, *including* saints, guides, and gurus, is on an evolutionary journey, along with our world, involving continual change.

The universe is *alive*, responding to our conscious activity. This book explores how this interaction occurs, and how we participate in this divine Trinity, either knowingly or unknowingly. We develop a working concept of a personal spirituality as possessed by each individual, employing extensions of philosophy and psychology in finding principles that you can apply for improving your life experience. We also draw from metaphysicians and mystics, from archetypal myths from millennia past, and from present-moment introspection.

This personal spirituality requires a new look at the psychology linking your thoughts and emotions. Both thought and emotion—messages of your head and heart, respectively—are necessary in the dialog with the Generative Principle. We will explore how these conscious activities are employed through cognitive and meditative practices for communing effectively with the Generative Principle. Essentially, this practice is an interaction between consciousness and subconsciousness, the latter being the personal and collective storage mechanism of the Generative Principle.

You may greatly benefit from an outside authority such as a therapist, spiritual leader, physician, marriage counselor, or financial advisor. However, relative to the Generative Principle, there are many things you can do for yourself, the most important of these being very simple. All of the great masters, such as Jesus, Buddha, and Lao Tse, spoke simple yet profound truths in very understandable language. They led exemplary lives without technical knowledge of the modern world. Only *you* can do your most consequential act, communing with the Generative Principle, for no one can do it for you.

What is life? What is the relationship between consciousness, the Generative Principle and experience? What is the balance between the masculine and feminine principles of creation in the New Trinity? How and why do the experiences of your life occur? What can you do to change things? These are questions that we will address as we journey forth hand-in-hand with the Generative Principle, unveiling your true nature as an incorruptible Spiritual Self, and providing a new perspective of your self-worth and competence.

Questions are included at the end of each chapter for your review, either in classroom, workshop, or individual study.

THE NEW TRINITY

CHAPTER 1

YOUR INNER
SPIRITUALITY

A New Awareness

The development of a personal spiritual identity presents us with some challenging questions. How can I, in my limited and imperfect human body with a history of mistakes and misdeeds, truly feel that I am a spiritual being? How can I feel good about myself and find inherent freedom with inner peace and joy? How can I learn to be free from fear and anxiety and experience a sense of connection with others? Our human and spiritual identities are not incompatible. As body and consciousness, they are both important perspectives to be explored in the process of realizing your total, holistic nature and improving your life experiences.

The good news is that you can develop and experience an awareness of your spiritual identity without an external authority, for it is something that you can do for yourself. In fact, there is no other way. Whatever your current situation in this world, you do not need to be *saved, anointed,* or *blessed* because inherently you already are a perfect spiritual being. You have qualities and capabilities of which you may not be aware.

You begin by developing a perspective distinguishing between your two simultaneous identities. You are a human being with a physical body imbedded in the world. At the same time, you are much more than that. You are capable of improving your life experiences *all by yourself.* It will require some dedication to learn about this new identity and how to use it, but the results will be worth the effort. The following diagram illustrates the alternative perspectives of self-identity.

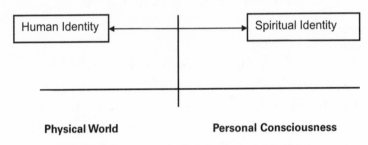

Figure 1. Alternative Perspectives of Human Identity

Your spiritual nature is not something to be found outside yourself. Contrary to the perspective of the old medical model, which is still believed by some neuroscientists, your consciousness is not contained within your brain or elsewhere in your body. It is a non-physical entity distinct from the material world, yet having *necessary* physiological reflections in your body as its medium for experience and expression. Many interactions between consciousness and the brain have been observed and measured in medical laboratories. Psychiatrist and neuroscientist, Daniel Siegel, in *The Mindful Brain* (2007) states: "We can say that the mind and brain correlate their functions, but we don't know the exact ways in which brain activity and mind function mutually to create one another. It is too simplistic to say merely that 'brain creates the mind' as we know that the mind can activate the brain...These associations are just that: not causal proofs, but two dimensions of reality that ultimately cannot be reduced to one another" (24). The position of this book is that consciousness *lives in the moment* outside of time and space, but observes the movement of earthly developments.

Since each of us has a physical body involved in earthly experiences, it is easy to incorrectly consider *only* these material situations when forming our own identity. It requires an initial conceptual leap to understand and accept a non-physical consciousness, yet you will become more comfortable with this idea as we progress. A most valuable consequence of consciousness being complementary to the body is that appropriate activities of the mind can produce positive changes in human experience, especially in realizing characteristics of your spiritual nature. Such an approach does not in any way deny or discount human identity for it is an essential aspect of our composite being and our only means of expression.

There is a power and intelligence in the universe that acts in cooperation with your conscious mind, producing changes in your experience. In this book, it is referred to as the *Generative Principle*. This principle is not supernatural. It actually incorporates all the physical laws of the universe. This is not a new idea. Early cultures intuitively sensed the archetypical nature of this principle, incorporating it into their mythology as the *Goddess*. The traditional name in Western and near-Eastern cultures for a transcendental deity controlling earthly events is God. For our purposes, this term is intentionally avoided because it involves some concepts and religious trappings that do not apply, and are actually contrary, to ideas regarding the Generative Principle.

The Generative Principle differs greatly from the traditional concept of God as it is employed within Judaism, Christianity, and Islam. *She* is immanent, rather than remote, receptive to each of our beliefs, and non-judgmentally responsive to them in creating manifestations. The characteristics of receptiveness and responsiveness are customarily considered feminine, distinct from the traits assigned to the domineering, judgmental male God. Thus, it is appropriate for the

Generative Principle to be associated with the feminine aspects of the divine previously attributed to the mythical Goddess and, for brevity, we employ the feminine gender: *Her* or *She.*

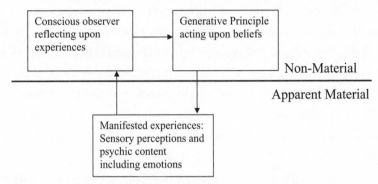

Figure 2. Interactions within the New Trinity

The Generative Principle is personally responsive to the conscious activity of each person, utilizing a person's specific beliefs—formed with conviction—to manifest worldly experiences. It is, therefore, very important to learn the language of the Generative Principle in order to create a better life. Emotions, as well as thoughts, are part of this language for, as we shall study, emotions are efficient indicators of those beliefs that we form.

The human body with its sensory mechanisms experiences apparent physical manifestations. Evaluating such experiences in consciousness, we form beliefs that are deposited within the Generative Principle. As illustrated in Figure 2, both consciousness and the Generative Principle interact in a non-material realm, producing the phenomena of the material world. These three components—consciousness, Generative Principle, and our resulting experiences—constitute the *New Trinity.* Perceptions of manifestations within the phenomenal world provide us with feedback from our personal beliefs. The Generative Principle is thus the exclusive unifier, providing mind/body integration in response to the agency of consciousness.

The transformation of beliefs into manifestations is somewhat analogous to the quantum mechanical process of converting waves into particles having material mass. For example, unseen electromagnetic waves in the old conventional television picture tube formed protons that caused illumination of the viewing screen. Niels Bohr termed this relationship the *complementary* principle. This is where an object, either wave or particle, having seemingly contradictory properties can be viewed by either perspective. In a similar manner, non-material consciousness and the material human brain and body are loosely complementary, but with a connection supported through the Generative Principle.

Although the Generative Principle is responsible for these manifestations, this formative action is in direct response to beliefs resulting from one's willful conscious evaluations and judgments. Creative action begins within our consciousness because, as conscious beings, we have a participatory relationship with the Generative Principle in the process of creation.

We do not create beneficial manifestations by *wishful thinking* or by the previously popular technique of "Positive Thinking." A different orientation toward and utilization of our spiritual nature is required to affect our experiences and bring about inner peace and joy. This approach puts aside human emotions, such as desire, anxiety, aversion, and fear, for these are not encountered within the spiritual orientation.

We come to understand that it is effective to consciously communicate new beliefs to the Generative Principle for Her to produce improved manifestations. We do not petition this source to provide earthly desires or to correct our misfortunes. Instead, we affirm what exists in our essential being. An improved experience naturally follows and is here referred to as the *Divine Child*, a product of the New Trinity. While working with the Generative Principle, it is important to practice patience, without specific expectations, since She responds *in her own time* with manifestations *of her own design*—and always in a most appropriate manner, yet not always according to our anticipation. Her intelligence is much greater than ours in determining what is most appropriate at any given time.

Our everyday experiences constantly demand of our attention, so in order to communicate with the Generative Principle it is best to clear our minds of what happened in the past or what we antici-pate for the future. Our spiritual being exists in the present moment; therefore, becoming aware of the *now* through mindfulness is a good starting place. In this book, we will learn a special type of meditation that brings us into the moment and allows us to focus on the goodness and freedom of our spiritual identity. Such practice will bring spiritual reality into our human experience.

A Spiritual Allegory

It is interesting to view the Generative Principle in the context of Her archetypical roots of the Paleolithic and Neolithic periods. Primitive man's understanding of the operation of this world was largely intuitive, providing lessons for us today through metaphor and analogy. The following allegory provides some insight into tech-niques for communicating with the Generative Principle:

More than fifteen thousand years ago a tribal Shaman holding a flickering stone oil lamp crawls into a limestone cave near the Dordogne River. Pausing for a rest after a half-hour venture through narrow passage, he feels inside his leather pouch, clutches with rev-erence the Goddess figurine carved from mammoth ivory and, as he realizes the importance of the task ahead, renewed purpose and vitality flow through him.

The crawlway opens at last into a modest-sized chamber with towering calcite columns. With reverence he marvels in awe as his meager light becomes lost in the darkness ahead. Assurance replaces apprehension and fear as he remembers that this mysterious cavity within Mother Earth is a source of new life. He withdraws the figurine of the Goddess from his pouch and presses it against his pounding heart. A feeling of thankfulness fills him in this privileged job of "seeding nature's womb" to provide continued abundance for his people.

Replenishing his lamp with animal grease, he sets it upon a rounded depression atop a stalagmite, illuminating an empty space on a flowstone wall bordered on each side by colorful paintings. He recalls, ten cycles of the sun past, his first viewing of this panorama of animal life—these drawings of bison, deer, mammoths, and horses. The previous Shaman of the tribe brought him, as a young initiate, into this restricted sanctuary instructing him in the mysteries of life's perennial renewal and his future part in this process.

Now, as that future becomes the present, he places his hands upon the wall, closes his eyes, and turns his vision to the hunt, the drama of man and beast, of struggle, death, and the promise of continued sustenance for the tribe. How different is the wild and frantic action of the outer world compared to the quiet serenity of this temple within the body of the Goddess.

In a trance-like state he moves his hands about the wall feeling every bump and crevice until, at last, excitement flows through him. The rounded object that he felt is no longer just a protrusion of stone, but is now in his mystic vision the shoulder of a living rhinoceros. Quickly, he pulls forth his lump of charcoal and begins to outline its body. In the course of several hours, he adds a horse, a few spears, and then deer. Feeling incomplete, he sketches a net-like pattern satisfying to him, yet whose exact meaning is beyond his conscious formulation.

Emotionally exhausted, he sinks to the floor with relief and gratitude for the consummation of his privileged task. Resting briefly before his departure, he plans his return within a few days when he will bring his three assistants carrying his pigments, torches, and amulets. After their ceremonial completion of the drawings in color, they will rejoice in the fertility of this earthen womb. A meditative ritual for release and detachment—disavowing personal accomplishment, yet affirming their linkage in the natural order—will precede their departure.

Four days later the entrance to the cave will be sealed for a ten-new-moon period of gestation while the Shaman and tribe dwell in a sense of celebration and thanksgiving, relying upon the nurturing reception of their seed and the subsequent generative process that progresses unseen. They will make new spears and optimistically engage in the daily hunt to feed the tribe.

Questions for Discussion

(1) What elements constitute the *New Trinity*?

(2) How does the Generative Principle compare with what you have previously considered as the generative forces of the universe? What is the origin of these previous concepts?

(3) Are you willing to explore a new pathway toward your spiritual identity?

(4) Does the spiritual allegory assist your understanding of the New Trinity in practice?

CHAPTER 2

ARCHETYPAL BASIS FOR THE NEW TRINITY

We live in a world of cycles, each having its own period lasting seconds, days, or millennia. My grandfather always consulted the lunar signs shown in the Farmer's Almanac before selecting a time for planting crops of north central Texas. He never realized that this tradition of lunar awareness began over seven thousand years before in Neolithic agrarian communities. His psychic roots and ours extend deep into human history, where imagery and symbolism continually repeat themselves. Seasons of planting and harvesting in the ancient agrarian cultures were of primary importance in the sustenance of life. In that dawn of civilization the cycles of natural phenomena were more carefully observed, given significant meanings, and periodically celebrated. They gave particular attention to cycles of the sun, its angular precession relative to the horizon, with phases of the moon having similar importance. The birth of each individual, marking the beginning of the human life cycle, was seen analogous to other periodic phenomenon within nature.

The Bronze Age cultures of the Eastern Mediterranean particularly recognized the perennial nature of all life, human and vegetable. In their celebrations of annual cycles, the fall seasonal decay of agricultural life and springtime revival symbolically corresponded to the death and rebirth of a male God of their mythology. Their ceremonies insured and celebrated fruition, where analogical reasoning linked both the animal and vegetable kingdoms through one principle of regeneration, represented in their culture as the Goddess (Frazier, 1963, 377—380).

The unity of all things, provided through one unknown, intelligent, and efficacious principle, was an idea originating in the earliest of mankind's ideological representations in early Paleolithic times. Although this concept of the divine Generative Principle has undergone many alterations and distortions, it is now cycling back to its original connotation as detailed in this book.

The Ethereal Goddess

An interesting society existed during Paleolithic times in Europe. Hundreds of scenes depicted in cave paintings showed sparse evidence of human aggression (Bahn and Vertut, 1988), suggesting a relatively peaceful period. Cave paintings, engravings, and sculptures from Southern France and Northern Spain provide a wealth of information about this culture, spreading eastward over the millennia as far as Siberia. This relic imagery consists primarily of animals, symbols, and an abundance of human, predominantly feminine, figures and representations.

The inner cave where paintings and engravings were most often found was not a place of habitation, but rather a *sanctuary* (Campbell, 1969, 66). In this sacred place for celebrating the principle of regeneration, feminine imagery was often utilized. Stylized feminine figures were engraved into cave walls or carved in stone, bone, or ivory. Large breasts extended, egg-shaped buttocks, and delineated vulvae or pubic triangles emphasized their fertility function (Gimbutas, 1989, 99-109). Hundreds of small statues of similar form, termed Goddesses, have been found throughout the Paleolithic Age and into the Bronze Age. This spiritual imagery suggests an important model for the generative

Figure 3. "Venus with Horn," Laussel Site, France

process relating how we, as individuals, interact with the formative powers of nature.

The Goddess figures symbolized womanhood's ability to
replenish the earth through annual seasons, the birth-life-death
cycles of their tribal members, and herds of animals coming and
going. These figures represent the workings of a feminine
Generative Principle. Through analogies with the lunar cycle—
well documented in the later Neolithic period—the principle of
regeneration also exists through the unseen emptiness between
death and new birth, in the period of darkness connecting the
seasons of fall and spring, and in that duration *between* the departure and return of the herd (Baring and Cashford, 1992, 18-22).

These beliefs of early prehistory revered life with its earthly
interdependencies, and the Goddess represented the great mys-

tery, requiring a veneration that inspired some of the world's first sculptural art, such as shown in Figure 3. Reporting on the period from 35,000 BC to 8,000 BC, Jacquetta Hawkes (1993, 54-59) stated: "The 'Venuses,' as they have been called, can be seen as the earliest religious symbols, since they seem to express a timeless sense of motherhood and fecundity."

This vanguard of religious ideas was *fundamental* rather than merely *primitive*, incorporating principles of life observed in the simplest of terms. The enduring concept of the Goddess flourished for at least 40 millennia. Hence we must conclude that it successfully met the psychic needs of this era. Tens of millennia prior to the advent of Buddha, Jesus, Muhammad, and other male spiritual leaders, Paleolithic societies recognized the presence of a power and intelligence beyond their own. The fact that this presence was represented only as feminine is significant beyond the mother representation.

Although it may be tempting to re-embrace the myth of the Goddess into our concept of the Divine, Joseph Campbell (Consineau, 1990, 204) cautioned us: "You cannot export myth, either through space or time." The Goddess myths were appropriate in millennia past but, as Campbell so often advocated, we must move forward to create our own myths. Still, in remembrance of the Goddess, there are elements of value from the ancients that can be incorporated into a mythology for our new millennium.

The Generative Principle as Soul

The Generative Principle was represented symbolically by imagery of the Goddess. Alternatively, you may choose to identify the immanent presence of the Generative Principle as your Soul. The Greek philosophers Pythagoras, Plato, and Aristotle introduced the term Soul in their writings over two and a half millennia ago. Yet, it is the later work of Plotinus that was significant in bringing this Hellenistic concept into Western philosophy. Born Egyptian of Greek culture in the third century AD, Plotinus moved to Rome. In his school there he developed an elaborate philosophy incorporating Soul as the link between the intelligible or spiritual and the material world. Thus, Soul became a philosophical replacement for the mythical Goddess. The writings of Plotinus (Armstrong, A. H., 1998, 175-222), as well as Aristotle, deeply influenced St. Augustine in forming his theology by modifying the interpretation of the trinity for the Western Catholic Church (Armstrong, Karen, 1994, 119-122).

The Generative Principle, interpreted as Soul, is receptive to your every thought, forming that web of inter-connectivity between your consciousness and your experience. The term *Goddess* is associated with an ancient era, whereas you may find Soul, rather than the Generative Principle, a more comfortable expression. Our society usually relegates the concept of Soul to the fields of religion or philosophy as an aspect of the individual continuing beyond earthly existence. Most concepts of Soul are generally ambiguous. Some dismiss it as an abstract concept or disregard it entirely as being of no importance. Most often, the concern with Soul is its disposition after death rather than its role during life.

The function of the Goddess, Soul, or Generative Principle has been obscured by our scientific way of thinking. We live in a society in which science has a near undisputed voice of authority, where observable or predicted cause-and-effect relationships are the constructs of scientific logic, and where we are expected to look for the *external* causes for our human circumstances. All branches of science, whether physical, biological, or behavioral, depend upon an observable series of events upon which to base their principles. This view of scientific determinism provides apparent validity for our dependence on external circumstances. Yet, all the principles of science, valid within the physical system, are transcended by a higher principle, that is, the creative expression of the feminine Generative Principle, Goddess, or Soul. This generative function lies between two parallel processes in play, the spiritual and the physical.

The generative function is assigned the feminine gender because its characteristics correspond to those of the feminine archetype represented by the Goddess. Erich Neumann, in his book *The Great Mother* (1972, 43), wrote of this archetype: "If we combine this body-world equation of early man in its first unspecified form with the fundamental symbolic equation of the feminine, woman = body = vessel, we arrive at a universal symbolic formula for the early period of mankind: Woman = body = vessel = world."

The feminine Generative Principle is the vessel, which is unconditionally receptive to your thoughts and feelings, and through Her creative medium incubates and becomes born as your worldly experience. In *Her* time and place She is always responsive, but never acquiescent. Her liquid expression provides present-moment spontaneity as well as uncertainty for the future. Thus, we find mystery and darkness in Her ways, a characteristic attributed to the Goddess or Great Mother of earlier cultures.

We egocentrically believe ourselves to be our life's directors, but when something disruptive happens, such as an accident or, perhaps, a compulsive action, we then seriously question what forces of unknown design are in control of our experience. Our usual rationalization for not being in control is that we are subjected to the will of other people, our genetic heredity, our childhood patterning, or to random chance; and, thereby, we are susceptible to the social and political impositions of our time. Such viewpoints provide easy justification for our human dilemmas because we can always point to an external cause. Seldom do we consider the Generative Principle as being involved. She continually and enduringly speaks to you through a multitude of worldly events including the ordinary, the exciting, the intimate, the traumatic, and the painfully debilitating. This book is about attending to these experiences orchestrated by the Generative Principle, finding deep meaning in them, and discovering a potential to improve the quality of your life.

You will never be able to control all the details of your life for they remain the choice of the Generative Principle. Eventually, you will find great relief in knowing and trusting that such details are being handled by a most competent source, and that with increasing proficiency you may control the inner quality of your life. You will soon gain a new perspective of yourself that will make this process much easier. As in the learning of any new language, practice is required for both understanding the messages of the Generative Principle and speaking your word to Her. Increasingly, you will find the tongue natural and familiar.

Balance of Gender within the Generative Equation

From analogies in biology, we know that the feminine gender does not act alone in the process of reproduction. Likewise, the metaphor of sexual union extends into metaphysical relationships with the divine, requiring a masculine component to balance the feminine in the generative equation. The Generative Principle does not give birth to her earthly manifestations in an arbitrary manner, and neither did She in the myths of prehistoric times. The progeny of her generative efforts include some representation of the masculine progenitor. Joseph Campbell expressed: "The world-generating spirit of the father passes into the manifold of earthly experience through the transforming medium—the mother of the world," (1972, 297).

Your conscious mind interacting with the Generative Principle activates this generative union. Consequently, experiences sprout from contents within the Generative Principle. But, an important concept developed within this book is that this formative process is influenced by new beliefs you create. The term *belief*, as used here, denotes an important concept with special meaning far beyond mere opinion. Beliefs designate personal subconscious content within the Generative Principle. Such content is here termed a *kernel*, a metaphor for a seed, as a kernel of corn.

In addition, from mathematics a kernel describes an equivalent that is mapped from one domain to another. *In our context, thought-judgments formed with conviction in the domain of consciousness map into kernels of belief within the Generative Principle that eventually transform into experiences.* Kernels are composed from those formative thoughts released from consciousness that underlie specific beliefs within the subconscious. These concepts are further developed in later chapters.

Some kernels generating your experience were brought with you into this world at birth—from some prior, unknown existence—so that you began your life with circumstance and direction, like a river upon which your boat moves with the current between the confines of the riverbanks. How was the course of your particular river chosen? And, what determines the occasions of calm waters or turbulence and the scenery along the banks? What freedom do you have in steering your boat through the strong current? We can never know all the answers, but we will later examine your freedom for thought and action and how your conscious activities influence the path of the current.

James Hillman, drawing from the myths of Plato's time, describes this destiny of human life by the "acorn theory," which provides an initial image corresponding to the life of each individual (Hillman, 1996). That which Hillman terms the "soul's code" in determining this image is analogous to the Generative Principle's utilization of kernels as described here. Acorns for Hillman pertain to life's overall course, whereas kernels relate to specific value judgments recorded within the Generative Principle. In his book, *The Soul's Code*, Hillman employs biographical data to illustrate how the character and patterns of famous lives cannot be totally explained simply by the influences of materiality, such as genetics, heredity, or social influence, which are the accepted answers of traditional science. Mythically speaking, we each have our *daemon* to guide us in our particular expression according to the acorn's pattern.

The mythology of prior millennia allegorically tells us about our relationship with the generative source. The occurrence of a written language during the Bronze Age allowed for the documentation of hymns and stories handed down from the oral tradition of earlier ages. One relevant myth pervading across numerous millennia involves the divine marriage of a young God with the Goddess. In these readings, we encounter that same fertility Goddess that we found engraved on cave walls and carved in ivory during the Paleolithic era and later represented with frescos and ceramics in the Neolithic era.

These stories describe a male God who is born of the Goddess and later unites with Her as consort-lover. The God dies and is lost to the underworld, but is resurrected to life and then reunited with Her. Relating the myth to the lunar cycle often associated with the Goddess, Baring and Cashford, in their scholarly work tracing the Goddess through history, stated: "She gives birth to her son as the new moon, marries him in the full moon, loses him to the darkness of the waning moon, goes in search of him as the dark moon, and rescues him as the returning crescent" (1992, 147).

Among the parallel meanings of the myth, the *son* of the Goddess symbolically represents you. As Her consort, you are the planter that tills the soil and drops the seed; She is the mother earth that nurtures the seed and perennially supplies the new harvest. Your creative effort with Her occurs as your consciousness forms new beliefs that are deposited within Her through the media of your subconscious mind. These contents are presented again to your awareness through experience by way of Her engendered response, the formless assuming experiential form.

You and I, whether male or female, have an identity analogous to the masculine God; that is, you are—we each are—the masculine God incarnate. In this capacity, we have a creative responsibility through our relationship with the Feminine Generative Principle. Realization of this process severs the imagined dependence upon the transcendental male God, the obsolete myth incorporated within most Western religions.

The creative spirit is integral to the consciousness of both men and women regardless of gender, sexual preference, or orientation. As the masculine God, it provides a balance with the feminine principle of the Goddess, and also is essential in comprising the complete whole. This cooperative balance, symbolically encompassing union of the masculine and the often-repressed feminine gender, constitutes the Sacred Marriage.

Our bodies arise through the same formative powers that form all earthly manifestations, returning again to the earth at the end of our tenure. In parallel, our embryonic conscious awareness emerges at birth along with this physical form and grows into awareness of a unique self-identity within the

human situation. Expressed thoughts and emotions are continually released from consciousness, leaving their residual kernel
within our subconscious, with subconscious mind being our personal reservoir within the Generative Principle. Thus, there are
two parallel cycles—physical and psychic—occurring simultaneously, from dust to dust upon Mother Earth, consciousness
mysteriously emerging, then returning to the Goddess.

The sacred marriage occurs through this archetypical interaction with the Goddess: The activity of conscious mind within each
individual is the masculine component of the universe, complementing and counterbalancing the Goddess in the generative equation. As expressed by Erich Neumann: "It is consistent with the
conscious-unconscious structure of opposites that the unconscious
should be regarded as predominantly feminine, and consciousness
as predominantly masculine. This correlation is self-evident
because the unconsciousness, alike in its capacity to bring to birth
and to destroy through absorption, has feminine affinities," and
further, "The system of ego consciousness is masculine. With it are
associated the qualities of volition, decision, and activity as contrasted with the determinism and blind 'drives' of the precon-
scious, egoless state" (Neumann, 1995, 125).

The creative activity of the Generative Principle, which produces worldly encounters, begins with the activity of conscious
mind. Therefore, your personal role in this universe is greater than
you may have imagined in altering the course of your experience.
The fruit of this union with the Generative Principle is enhanced as
you further recognize and exercise your individual spiritual identity.

The total generative function consists of two interdepen-
dent faculties, which are symbolically represented by the God
and Goddess as follows.

MASCULINE	FEMININE
Spirit	Generative Principle
consciousness	subconscious
active	passive
initiative	receptive
creator in thought	creatress in form

Our finite material existence is transitory, like each phase of the moon. But, the Goddess lives on perpetually, encompassing all perennial variations within Her changeless whole. The agricultural communities of the Near East saw the new moon as an assurance of the seasonal harvest and viewed the return of the male God as the seed-bearer necessary for continued renewal of plant life. Resurrection of the God from his underground exile was occasion for a spring celebration that has been continued in various forms throughout many cultures over the millennia.

In his epic, *The Golden Bough*, Sr. James Frazer (1963, 161-169) termed the union of the Goddess and God as the "Sacred Marriage," and commented upon the annual celebration: "Is it not likely that in certain festivals of the ancients we may be able to detect the equivalents of our May Day, Whitsuntide, and Midsummer celebrations, with this difference, that in those days the ceremonies had not dwindled into mere shows and pageants, but were still religious or magical rites, in which actors consciously supported the high parts of Gods and Goddesses?"

The male Gods involved in the sacred marriage were *mortal* divinities, which is to say that they were short-lived compared to the Goddess, sharing the finite span of all human life. Yet, their earthly incarnation was perennially recurring, born of the eternal Goddess as a necessary aspect of Herself *required* for procreation. Whereas, the masculine God is likened unto the transitory phases of the moon, the Goddess is analogous to the whole sphere. She is always present, though She might reveal only a crescent manifestation at any time with the rest of herself being obscured from our view.

The Divine Child

As conscious mind embraces and affirms goodness, peace, and beauty, an impregnating effect is produced in subconsciousness. This union of gender, as a sacred marriage, produces a special form of creation that reflects the inherent divine nature of each individual. *The Divine Child emerges as the realized spiritual being, a joyous creation within consciousness.* This is a third aspect of the divine trinity within the human psyche, in parallel to physical expression, likened to a visitation of the Holy Spirit.

Correspondingly, physical as well as psychic representations of the Divine Child occur, varying in form and expressing the boundless artistry of the Goddess through individuals and society. As a human expression, the child grows, flourishes, and then dies away like the allegorical male God of the Neolithic. As Gautama Sakyamuni became the Buddha and Jesus became the Christ, so each individual can cultivate his or her spiritual nature with no intermediary, demonstrating spiritual nature through the works of goodness and beauty.

The creative variations exhibited in our material world insure that each pattern of goodness is never exactly repeated. The body of the corporeal child is transitory, appropriate for its own moment, and beyond our permanent possession. Yet, thought-by-thought, we build upon the collective unconsciousness, and through each word and deed we construct the cultural heritage of this earth.

We need to discover what conditions are necessary to bring the Divine Child and its epiphany into our lives. The answer lies in rediscovering and embracing our intrinsic spiritual nature and *living* this truth of being while communing with the Generative Principle. By turning within to the heart of our spiritual being, as through meditation, we can find peace, love, and harmony as qualities of our divine nature. As we express these qualities in our lives through the creativity of the Generative Principle, we can feel and existentially encounter the unlimited dimensions of ecstasy—for example, observing the shades of a beautiful sunset varying from moment to moment in the dusk of a cool evening, or walking hand-in-hand with a loving companion sharing intimate thoughts.

The consummation of the Sacred Marriage with the Generative Principle occurs with the mental realization of inner divinity. This alchemical union involves consciously realizing our inherent goodness and our connectedness with all others, accepting this as the truth of our being, relying upon powers beyond our limited ego-oriented self, and then releasing these thoughts to the Generative Principle. The Generative Principle acts upon each seed of goodness we plant, producing a splendid multiplicity for our harvest. The process, further examined in later chapters, is as simple and as mysterious as its agricultural analogy.

Ascent of the Ego

If societies of past millennia once had such an inner perspective regarding the nature of things, how and when was this lost? Why did opposition displace alliance and harmony and obscure the holistic vision involving the Goddess? Numerous explanations have been offered, such as changing climatic conditions and animal husbandry replacing agriculture, as well as cultural advancements such as the development of written language that began significant transformations with profound effects. Additionally, cataclysmic social developments as described below combined to provide a valid accounting from the physical perspective. However, social consequences begin their genesis within the human mind. An important question, then, is: what metamorphoses occurred in human consciousness to underlie this major transformation of human identity and provide the assent of an overriding human ego?

Human consciousness likely followed some evolutionary trail during its long development from that period of several million years ago when the first humanoid skeleton remains were deposited to become fossilized. Yet, the majority of such developments for Homo Sapiens occurred during the past 100,000 years. The following discussion relates not only to history, but also to developments occurring within each person from time of birth.

Erich Neumann affirmed in his book *The Origins and History of Consciousness* that the individual in primitive societies experienced a "collective" identity and did not yet differentiate personal self from worldly surroundings. A term for this state of awareness is called *uroboros*. It is depicted by the symbol of a circular snake or reptile biting its own tail. Self-image, at this stage, is absorbed within the collective whole of nature and the tribe in a psychic process termed the *participation mystique* in which there is little discrimination between one's self and the swirl of experience.

As conscious awareness progressed from the primordial undifferentiated stage, the individual began to recognize a distinction between itself and the environment, but still experienced an engulfing dependence upon unseen powers beyond its own. When individual consciousness discriminates itself from the collective whole, it feels an "undeniable sense of deficiency that attaches itself to the emancipated ego...This emancipation is in reality the fundamental liberating act of man that releases him from the yoke of unconscious-

ness and establishes him as an ego, a conscious individual"
(Neumann, 1995, 120). The Goddess myths provided a psychological security in which the individual was engulfed like a fish swim-
ming in an embryonic ocean. Breaking free was a necessary step in
the development of individuality. The emancipation process sometimes involved a violent reaction that resulted in such myths as the
hero slaying the dragon.

The Generative Principle incorporates the subconscious
mind so that consciousness can never escape this underlying sub-
stratum from which it arose and to which it perennially returns.
It is necessary for the conscious mind to distinguish itself from
the subconscious in order for it to exercise and strengthen its
vital properties of discrimination and volition. Unfortunately,
the evolution of an independent self-consciousness resulted in a
distorted view in which the human body was the primary identity. As a result, individualized consciousness incorporated a
worldly ego excluding its nonmaterial spiritual nature. Further
development of conscious discrimination was accomplished by
increased identification with the material self and decreased
association with primordial connections, including the Goddess.

Despite this, the subconscious has continued to inform
receptive individuals of their spiritual identity, usually during
times of quiet and reflective meditation. Humans are unique
among other life forms in that we have developed a self-awareness that, with intention, can acquaint us with our spiritual
nature. However, this nature may remain obscured by ego.

The ego has a material orientation in contrast to a spiritual
one. It tends to enhance itself by inflation and domination
through animal-like behavior following models observed elsewhere in nature. An infantile, material-based identity grows
through power and possessions, and by imposing its will over

others.   Conquest and domination characterize this phase of development, producing an oppressive era for humanity. The ego can sometimes portray the archetypal dominant male regardless of gender. As related in the following section, archaeological evidence indicates that during fifth and second millennia BC such a phase in self-identity occurred, producing a shift of cataclysmic proportion. However, such changes also occur during the growth of each person between birth and conscious maturity.

Why is it so difficult to recapture the spiritual orientation appearing in earlier millennia? Why does the great shift to ego consciousness still linger with us today? The answers lie in human self-identity. In our very materialistic society, we too often view ourselves from the *outside-in*, rather than from the *inside-out*. We see our environment and ourselves from the eyes of our human body in an objective, scientific way. This physical-world perspective is not incorrect. Indeed, it is very important for us to register the material circumstances that surround us. Problems arise when this is the *only* perspective we have.

Some earlier scientists erroneously informed us that conscious activity was only an electrical activity in the brain and nervous system (Ornstein, 1986, 81-125). Some still maintain this position, but more recently numerous investigations indicate how conscious activity changes neurological structures (e.g., Siegel, 2007). It is consciousness that is self-adaptive with correlations reflected in the brain. Your body and its effects are demonstrations of the Generative Principle's creativeness, consequences initiated through consciousness. Your consciousness is a non-material entity under your control that cannot be contained and measured in a scientific laboratory.

We live in a material culture where values are often portrayed in terms of position, power, and money. Nature is fre-

quently viewed as something to be overcome and exploited for
the good of mankind. Focus on material identity is made at the
expense of spiritual identity. Inevitably, problems arise when *self-
esteem* is linked only to the evaluation of physical experiences.

An alternative to this dilemma of the ego is to learn to view
our self from the inside-out—from the subjective perspective of
a *conscious being*—and know that our identity is much greater
than our physical senses can determine. The sense of self-worth
increases enormously as we realize our spiritual being as the true
nature of consciousness. We find great comfort and confidence in
the Generative Principle by relying on Her as our co-creator.

Birth of the Domineering Male God

According to some archeologists, beginning in the middle of
the fifth millennium BC a great disruption of apocalyptic propor-
tions was imposed upon many of the Goddess cultures of prehistoric Europe. Indo-Europeans from the steppe region of southern Russia rode horses, unknown in Europe since the ice age, and
bore weapons of war designed for fighting that were superior to
the hunting implements of their victims. The invaders came in
waves of destruction and conquest for almost two millennia,
traveling initially to the southwest through the rich Danube
Valley, and invading the peace-loving, Goddess-worshipping cultures. The unarmed agriculturalists were no match for the
mounted warriors atop strange, towering animals thundering
through their streets. Such events provide analogy of some
actions that continue today. The Goddess cultures did endure in
some regions through this period of turmoil and provide a perspective contrasting to the invaders.

The social tradition of the invader sharply contrasted with the overrun cultures of old Europe. The leaders of the invaders likely were warrior chiefs who ruled a hierarchical, patriarchal culture in which females held an inferior role. Domination through power differentiated between those of greater and lesser might. Women had less physical strength and cultures with fewer defenses became subordinates. Respect for human life and possession of others was secondary to the quest for power.

The invaders left no symbols of their religious beliefs until the latter half of the fourth millennium BC, at which point engravings upon upright monoliths, termed *selae*, pictured warrior Gods with their weaponry, horses, and symbols of the sun. These symbols were very different from those of the Goddess society. Solar symbols, circles, and radiating suns continued through the prehistory of Indo-Europeans and into the recorded myths that describe a *God of the Shining Sun*.

Eventually, God became a dominant, male figure isolated in the sky as remnant of the Sun God, passing wrathful judgment upon and vindictively punishing those lesser mortals below. He was a God demanding worship in return for rewards, a transcendent God of separation rather than an immanent one of unification. In brief, he was a *God with an ego*.

The contrasting religious outlooks between the peaceful Goddess culture and the conquering Indo-Europeans imply two divergent perspectives of life. Recognition of the Goddess as representing the generative source of all earthly manifestations implies a *connection* of each individual with this source. The invading warrior, *disconnected* from the source, forcefully extorted his needs through personal abilities. He saw a limited universe rather than a bountiful one, where the power of the individual determined the haves and the have-nots. The idealized man with ultimate power, set *apart* from the rest, was elevated to god-like stature.

Many early Europeans were of an agrarian culture that viewed the abundance of the earth, including human life, as the divine nature of the Goddess made manifest. Thus, they considered the earth and themselves to be sacred. Such blessings of the epiphany were *shared in a spirit of cooperation* with each individual of the tribe. All worldly goodness, as the early Europeans well knew, perennially arose and declined like the crops in the field.

In contrast, the stereotypical invader saw the good things of the earth to be *taken as personal acquisitions*. A significant dichotomy was established between the image of the *self* and the *other*. These invaders, with no regard for a generative life source, viewed nature as an enemy, something to be overcome. Their material self-identity was based on strength, skill, possessions, and ability to prolong life. Greed, avarice, anxiety, disappointment, fear, and anger all result from this perspective. This attitude also resonates with activity sometimes encountered in today's society in the form of malevolent dictators, avaricious politicians, combative business practices, and selfish individual behavior.

The warrior-leader, hailed, idolized, or despised as the conquering hero, displaced the Goddess, initiating a new paradigm that continued in degrees throughout subsequent millennia. Although we may disfavor him as selfish and brutal, he is an early representation of that hero archetype which exists within each of us. The warrior-leader could have never occurred if a prototype had not existed within each subconscious mind. The archetypal Zeus, for example, can be recognized today in the aggressive and decisive person seeking authority and power (Bolen, 1989, 43-71). Yet these aggressive characteristics, when applied constructively, have beneficial application in society, providing a balance for other archetypes.

Two polar-opposite perspectives within the psyche's awareness lead to self-esteem: spiritual realization and material successes. Today, we often find ourselves caught somewhere in-between these two. The spiritual perspective is diminished if one's self-worth depends solely upon acquiring external things. The satisfaction of being an integral part of the generative whole, contrasts with the ego-centered position involving self-importance and physical gratification.

Everyone has an ego because we all have human bodies through which we operate on this earth. Self-image is egotistical only to the degree in which self-evaluation is confined solely to material values. This identity devalues loving relationships, the appreciation of beauty, and peace of mind. A worthy new-millennium paradigm will look beyond the ego's worldly agenda, reconnect us with the Generative Principle through a new spiritual identity, and produce the Divine Child for our age. But first, we must understand the unlimited potential within our own mind.

Questions for Discussion

(1) What is the oldest of religious symbols, and what did it represent?

(2) Why is the generative source described as feminine? How do you relate to terms such as Goddess, Soul, and Generative Principle?

(3) Do you recognize some aspects of your experience as being beyond observable cause-and-effect relationships?

(4) How do you feel about being the co-creator of your experiences?

(5) How would you describe the emergence of the human ego?

(6) How would you like the Divine Child to appear in your life?

CHAPTER 3

DYNAMICS OF CONSCIOUSNESS

The holistic perspective considers the evolution of both the material and spiritual as a parallel development: Human individuality has a temporal history as a component of the material world that has emerged through a physical evolution, whereas individuals are still developing in terms of consciously recognizing their essential nature[1]. The seat of your spiritual being is your non-material conscious mind, existing only moment-by-moment. This chapter examines communication with the Generative Principle in terms of interactions of consciousness and subconsciousness, and traces early recognition of the masculine and feminine aspects of divinity.

Evolution of Consciousness

Ancient and primitive societies, pondering how life began, formed creation myths, the meanings of which were handed down through generations. Across cultures, myths contain common themes. Formed independently, these recurrences appear to have originated within the collective unconsciousness. Thus, creation myths may be examined as projections from the cosmic subconscious mind, reflecting the origin of conscious life through allegory.

Among the numerous metaphors employed in creation myths—the birth of light out of darkness, for example—symbolizes the awakening of creation and the dawn of life. In other myths, the sphere (circle or egg) symbolizes the inclusive origin of the universe. (Interestingly, the term *cosmic egg* was revised in the cosmological theories in the twentieth century to represent the singularity that expanded with the *Big Bang*.)

Predominately, this original primitive unity was divided by gender as principal opposites, typically into the Earth Mother and Father Sky as, for example, by several Native American tribes, or as World Parents. Themes involving such types of complementary separation are common to the creation myths of many cultures. These World Parents correlate with the psychic components previously discussed—the mother figure being the Generative Principle incorporating subconsciousness and the father figure being consciousness. Yet, in the dawn of mankind individual consciousness was not separate and differentiated from collective unconsciousness.

The primeval Father was still submerged within the fluidic whole of the cosmic egg, with only primitive discrimination of opposites such as good and bad. Manifestations reflected the seemingly arbitrary laws of nature. Early human identity was confounded within the environment of the animal kingdom prior to the development of self-consciousness, and life caught in a Darwinistic struggle for survival. Individual consciousness emerged from the cosmic egg, providing generative subconscious source with new means of expression through the willful activity of Her offspring. This primordial development provided our lineage and inherent nature.

Early cultures held the Goddess in reverence as the creative principle of earthly manifestations. Sometimes the masculine and feminine functions were combined in Goddess imagery, resulting in an androgynous being. Thus, depictions of the Goddess occasionally had masculine as well as feminine characteristics, such as an elongated, phallic-like neck. An interpretation of this symbolism is that evolving conscious self-awareness was still closely embodied within the collective whole. An *a priori potentiality* for independent consciousness must have existed in order for its emergence from the amorphous whole. A great evolutionary step occurred, and is still occurring, for us to consciously recognize our agency of free will, original goodness, and the connection of love in characterizing our inherent spirituality.

We know through the study of biological sciences that the most primitive life forms had regulatory intelligence—present in even one-cell creatures—accepting nutrients, but avoiding toxins, with elementary discrimination. Internal signals initially were communicated by fluidic means, then blood through the circulatory system, later nerves, and eventually a brain. The early brain provided a seat of awareness, but rendered limited capability for judgment and certainly not self-awareness prior to the development of the more advanced human brain. The Generative Principle systematically orchestrated this gradual evolutionary process, bringing forth ever greater and complex means for life's expression.

Volitional consciousness, with self-realization, requires an appropriate means for physical manifestation. This was accomplished by evolutional developments such as the elaborate brain structure that we now possess. From this dual perspective of material and non-material, we might say by analogy that our brain serves as a horse upon which consciousness, as we understand it, rides to transport itself in thought into our human experience.

As we need legs to walk, eyes to see, and vocal anatomy to speak and express ourselves, we need brain functions to reflect and respond with volition in human experience. It is beyond our understanding to know if non-material consciousness can exist and operate if deprived of its special and temporal reference by death of the human body. The emphasis of this book is upon the *here and eternal now* of our immediate existence with its immanent connection with the Generative Principle, and in realizing that we emerge as a projection from Her and are never separated from Her. We may find ease with the Zen poem (Blyth, 1942, 173):

The water flows, but back into the oceans;
The moon sinks, but is ever in Heaven.

We require our physiological mechanisms to inform us of, and to participate in, our personal manifestation. All of our thoughts and emotions are correlated with and reflected within this material realm through a marvelous synchronized process. Our consciousness and physiology coordinate to provide the means for experience and expression. Due to this physiological correlation, neurologists continue to search for our conscious identity within our body. These investigations are not in error for they reveal the necessary biological conditions for conscious expression in the human body[2]. But, these alone are not sufficient conditions. *Correlation does not imply causation.*

Your Conscious Being

Consciousness is like a large mansion with many rooms in which you may dwell, one at time, with each window revealing a unique viewpoint. Here, you may observe your external, human experience, or your internal thoughts and imagery. Your fundamental conscious awareness forms a stationary vantage point by which your world parades. A very special and basic awareness peculiar to all humans is self-consciousness, the presence of that entity which we know as our self. Basic postulates addressed throughout this book regarding consciousness—also referred to as spirit— are that consciousness is non-material and exists only in the moment, and that consciousness and manifested body interact through the media of the Generative Principle.

Three fundamental activities of conscious mind are *differentiation*, *discrimination*, and *decision*, all acting upon the most primary and defining property of consciousness: *awareness*. These activities are interrelated. To direct your awareness in the process of differentiation is, itself, a decision, and decisions cannot be made without some awareness of and discrimination among options. For example, I do not select a book from the shelf until I scan the titles within my field of interest.

Personal awareness can come from your five senses, remembrances, intuitions, dreams, or visualizations. Each person, through differentiation, is free to shift his or her attention among these with freedom to alter attention and make related decisions. Coupled with discrimination, volition or will to decide is a most precious attribute of consciousness.

Through your volition, you continually decide whether to continue reading the sequential words of this book or to stop and reflect upon how they relate to your life. Considering all the options of your awareness as available choices, each focus of your attention itself becomes a decision, although you may attend to several channels of awareness simultaneously. For example, while reading you may notice a sensation of thirst and decide to get a glass of water. As you walk to the kitchen, you might become aware of the spatial surroundings and hear the radio playing while still being conscious of your thirst as the purpose for your journey.

Your conscious freedom to make decisions is the most important and sacred aspect of your being as this autonomous ability establishes your creative role as the masculine God incarnate. It is by means of this ability to act through intent and purpose that you balance the Generative Principle in your Sacred Marriage. The Generative Principle is responsive, rather than initiatory. Her decisions, quite different from yours, involve deductive selections for manifestation in demonstrating the content of your subconscious mind through experience. In order to most effectively use your sacred ability, it is necessary to understand how the functions of discrimination and decision interrelate with other conscious faculties. This knowledge also facilitates your communication with the Generative Principle, both in speaking to Her and understanding Her response to you.

Functions of Consciousness

Thinking, as considered here, is a *directed conscious movement* within the field of awareness, accomplished under your control. Decisions made, either initially or following contemplation, are your means of directing awareness. Thinking commonly involves mental symbols substituted for the actual experience, in which the abstraction of language—characters, names, icons, ideas, concepts, and other representations—is used instead of the physical thing itself. For example: When you hear comments such as, *Remember the musical show that I told you about? Well, I got us great seats, and our friends Henry and Nancy are coming with us*, the words are abstractions used in thinking, and represent people, events and actions. Reasoning, analysis, accounting, and idea formulation are types of thinking which employ the abstraction of symbols and transport awareness beyond physical sensation. Thought-decisions then occur as a mental *reflection upo*n physical events or objects within awareness.

Reasoning and logical thinking are valuable tools of consciousness, but alone do not form the passions and essence of life.

Thinking is not confined to intellectual pursuits. The artist applying color to the canvas, the dancer moving her body in inter-pretation of the music, the pianist playing the music, the basketball player dribbling the ball down the court between opponents all involve types of directed movements within a field of awareness. Thus, all engage some degree of thinking, although seemingly auto-matic actions also occur due to training and conditioning. Our sub-conscious mind assists in habitual actions such as driving an automo-bile and listening to music with minimal reflection required. Correspondingly, there are many types of intelligence depending upon the mode of awareness through which one operates[3].

Beyond thoughts are *emotions* and *feelings,* clothing our pas-sions and providing the zest for life, as in our exclamations, *I am so excited that you bought the tickets and I feel enchanted when I hear their music.* Your emotional nature is one characteristic that distin-guishes the action of your mind from the logic of a computer. Your joy, anger, peace, sadness, thanksgiving, fear, love, guilt, and other emotions are *human* responses. *Feelings*, such as excite-ment, are the physical manifestations of your emotions felt with-in your body, while *emotions* are cognitions within your conscious mind. For instance, when I feel extremely anxious about the out-come of a financial situation, I sense a discomfort through my whole upper body. I can rationally *know* of the anxiety, but it is my body that *feels* it.

Emotions are ancillary to mental concepts or to external events. For example, I feel exuberant if I have an exciting idea, a thrilling experience, or a stimulating encounter. Many of our emo-tions seem to surface automatically, concurrent with a physical event. If a bear were to lunge at me in the woods, I would likely respond with spontaneous alarm. These emotions that appear to occur immediately are here termed immediate emotions, with their importance addressed in greater detail in Chapter 6.

Immediate emotions arise prior to conscious reflection upon that which is perceived. This conscious perception is a result of either sensory perception or the imagery of the mind. For instance, a physical occurrence such as a song playing may remind one of a meaningful event of the past. Prior to reflection upon this past event, some *immediate emotion* will occur. These emotions that immediately arise with no reflection contribute to the total mood. Immediate emotions are of special importance, as we shall see, because they are efficient indicators from the Generative Principle of the significance underlying each psychic experience.

The Generative Principle is the source of all human experience, including physical manifestations, memory, dreams, and immediate emotions arising in response to physical events. Instincts, impulses and urges, similar to immediate emotions, are also incidents originating from the Generative Principle, often with responses in the body. Although we attribute some mental phenomena to subconscious origin, the subconscious mind is here considered as contained within the Generative Principle as discussed below[4].

As you converse with the Generative Principle in the *reflective* case, the creative order within consciousness is initially thoughts (metaphorically, the *head* level), accompanied, secondly, by emotions (the *heart* level). This order is reversed for unreflective events where the Generative Principle augments Her messages through your immediate emotions in response to the experience. The difference is whether you are *imparting* or *receiving* the message. As in any conversation, the sequence alternates. We do not speak to the Generative Principle as we might to an external, transcendent God for She is internal, immanent, and pervasive—not as a remote object, but as the *very ground* of subject itself.

All activities of consciousness have their own reality in the phenomenological sense, and subjectively are just as valid as the physical, measurable universe. Some of the most enlivening of our experiences may occur in the realm of the non-material. Our dreams and visions, sudden bursts of imagination, and emotions such as joy, surprise, anxiety, hope, fear, sadness, and anger, all contribute to the vitalization that keeps life interesting. We hear that our emotions and intuitions are not rational, which may be true according to some definition, but the word *rational* is merely a descriptive construct of language. As we shall later determine, there is reason behind every emotion, though sometimes beyond our awareness. Rational thinking and logic are valuable and accepted by science because they allow us to theorize and form the mental analog of an orderly universe. But, these types of thinking hold no inherent status of superiority relative to other modes of consciousness.

Generative Principle

Pioneers of psychology, including Freud and Jung, postulated the existence of the *subconscious mind* to explain phenomena of behavior appearing to originate from prior experience. The concept of a subconscious mind is important in explaining the response of consciousness toward past experiences because conscious mind exists only within the instantaneous moment and has no storage mechanism for memories. For example, if someone automatically reacts with fear toward dogs without apparent reason, it is assumed that they are conditioned by a previous experience that is now preserved only within subconsciousness.

Subconscious mind, as a theoretical and arbitrary hypothesis of psychology, is valuable for explaining psychic phenomena other than memories. For example, what is the source of imagination, dreams, intuitions, everyday values, and sudden impulses? All of these familiar phenomena appear to be injected into awareness from some outside source, generally assumed to be subconscious mind. In this book, the unseen and immeasurable source of these phenomena is postulated to be the subconscious mind. However, the subconscious mind, in turn, is postulated to lie within the Generative Principle, and serves as our primary source of memory, plus our personal repository containing things forgotten, released, or repressed from consciousness. As consciousness and subconsciousness[5] interchange information, they must be of the same non-material substance. Consequently, without the physical dimensions of time and space, they have no localization in the body or anywhere else. *Subconscious mind* provides a useful concept in exploring functional interactions with consciousness, yet the term has no more intrinsic meaning than the idiomatic *black box* of systems analysis, and is so utilized.

Although we usually think of the subconscious mind in a possessive sense, as for example my subconscious, it is actually a collective mechanism within the Generative Principle that has an aspect singular to each of us. She utilizes all subconscious contents to form universal experiences, including a personal experience created specifically appropriate for each person. She produces particular experiences—manifesting individual content, including the physical as well as mental. She acts impartially without judgment, deductively forming specific manifestations from subconscious content.

Our destiny, as the course of pending manifestations, is subject to modification by new thoughts that are held with conviction and transformed into *beliefs*. In this book the familiar term *belief* is utilized specifically for subconscious content. We have conscious *opinions*, but the term belief is exclusively reserved for contents of subconsciousness. That is, beliefs are formed from thoughts *released* from the conscious mind and composed from that which has been held as conscious *conviction*. Particular convictions, incorporating thought-judgments passed into subconsciousness, are referred to as *kernels of belief*. These kernels remain there as mini-archetypes to become manifest.

The Generative Principle does not produce specific manifestations for every casual and transitory conviction, as in the speculation *I might win the lottery next week*. Rather, She responds to the *inductive reduction* of your numerous convictions—to more general and inclusive evaluations such as, *I lead a life filled with prosperity*. She then selects the appropriate, particularized experience to demonstrate this prosperity, whether it is monetary gain, a new personal relationship or creative achievement. Kernels of belief are always formative, but sprout into specific experiences only as directed through the intelligence of the Generative Principle. Thus, experiences are specifications born of conviction. Conscious thoughts and emotions *converge* in the Generative Principle to form kernels of belief. These kernels, in turn, *diverge* in the formation of manifold manifestations, incorporating beneficial values into your beliefs.

The transformation of belief into manifestation by the Generative Principle, verifiable by observation, bridges the gap between mind and experience. We adopt a fatalistic viewpoint when we announce: *The universe has done it to me again*, or *It was God's will that this happened*. It is our personal pattern within the Generative Principle that determines our experience, and it is we who can alter this pattern through conscious thought leading to new beliefs. Although we often have limited methods for changing our momentary circumstances, we can always exercise choice in our responses.

It is often difficult to accept that there is something outside of awareness and beyond our control that directs events affecting us. We may question the fairness of the universe when we consider that patterns within the Generative Principle, determining much of our personal experience, *came with us* into this lifetime. How and why we will never know. We work hard toward objectives, but sometimes fail due to circumstances beyond our control. We feel great consternation as a consequence of disturbing and painful situations, having no idea of their origins.

> Examining existing convictions and understanding how we fashion new ones through thoughts and emotions are primary tasks in learning the language of the Generative Principle.

Conditions defining the bounds of our experience are termed by some existential philosophers as *facticity* or *contingencies*. Such conditions include our physical being with its continuing biography, along with historical and cultural factors. These contingencies characterize our human existence and the limits of our physical freedom, yet they provide the framework for new decisions. We work within these conditions, ideally, with acceptance and appreciation of each opportunity.

Fortunately, we can change patterns within our personal aspect of the Generative Principle through conscious thoughts and emotions that lead to new beliefs. Realization of a potential to improve quality of life and provide more satisfying experiences provides us with a more positive outlook upon the world. Forming convictions leading to new and favorable beliefs is, therefore, important among conscious actions, and most fruitful in communication with the Generative Principle. Significant changes in the phenomenal world will occur as a result of shifts in the collective subconscious mind, or *soul of the world*, borrowing a phrase from Robert Sardello (1992, 15-31). However, this occurs only as our individual conscious actions make their incremental contributions, with every thought being important.

Questions for Discussion

(1) How do you view the interaction of consciousness and brain activity?

(2) What is the difference between immediate and reflective emotions and what value are they?

(3) Where is the location of subconscious mind? What functions does it perform?

(4) How do kernels of belief differ from opinions?

(5) How do your individual thoughts affect world conditions?

Notes

[1] Stuart Kauffman gives an important exposition of evolution, emergence, and conscious agency from a physical perspective in his book, *Reinventing the Sacred* (2008).

[2] The neurological viewpoint is exemplified by the work of Antonio Damasio, such as *The Feeling of What Happens*. Dr. Damasio does appreciate the continued mysteries of consciousness.

[3] Harvard psychologist, Howard Gardner described the variety of mental capabilities, beyond the traditional IQ test, in what he calls his *theory of multiple intelligences* (Gardner, 1983).

[4] The Generative Principle has similarities to David Bohm's *Implicate Order* that provides a common ground for both consciousness and matter, (Bohm, 1980, 248-271), where the *Implicate Order* produces each explicit content of our conscious experience, and our awareness of it in the material world is an *Explicate Order*.

[5] The term *subconsciousness* is used here in preference to *unconsciousness* because the prefix *sub-* denotes *below*, whereas *un-* denotes *not*. The content of our subconscious mind is beyond or below our conscious awareness, yet it is accessible to the Generative Principle in providing Her manifestations. Beyond this matter of semantics, the usage of subconsciousness and unconsciousness in most psychological literature is equivalent.

CHAPTER 4

THE STRUCTURE OF CONSCIOUSNESS

Categories of Conscious Judgment

You live in only one moment, the moment of *now*. In the now, you may reflect upon the lessons of the past or plan for the future. However, to apply the lessons from the past or to work toward goals of the future, you always operate in the *here and now*. The past and present can never be more than the imagery drawn into this present moment. You are aware of time, but live in *immediate* time, an instant of the manifested world.

You continually differentiate by selecting and reflecting upon an object within awareness, whether it is another person, idea, or experience, and inevitably make some discriminating judgments about it. These *fundamental judgments* fall into three basic categories: (1) how much you like or dislike it, (2) how you associate with it, and (3) whether or not you accept it. We refer to these three categories as *quality*, *association*, and *acceptance*. Quality and association combine to form your *evaluation*. The three judgments are not independent, but generally have some conditional relationship between one another. Thus, *all evaluations are intentional*, which is to say, they are *about something* in experience.

Let us explore the concept of *acceptance* with an example. I hear a tune on the radio that sounds annoying to me. Then, I recall it being popular during a period in which I was having a difficult relationship. I might *tune it out* of my awareness, or *negate it*, to relieve a painful memory and turn my attention elsewhere. Or, I may allow my mind to reflect beyond that period of time. Through the *freedom of differentiation*, often supported with minimum contemplation, we are able to attend to and choose between the multitude of sensations and options within awareness. The subtle decision of acceptance is often not a rational consideration but, instead, is a very subjective and sometimes immediate determination made through a confluence of personal values.

Your discriminations regarding both *quality and association* made for everything that comes into your awareness, beyond the fixation of a Zen experience, are hereafter referred to as *evaluations*. Whenever you have a successful venture, e.g., obtaining an academic degree, completing a project at work, finding the mate of your desires, losing 20 pounds, or learning to play a musical instrument, your sense of self worth is enhanced. You announce, "I am successful," as a *quality* judgment associated with your human self. But, if nothing you attempt seems to work, you may think, *I can never do anything right, thus devaluing yourself*.

In judgments of quality, measures range from good to bad, favorable to unfavorable, or *for me to against me*, and all of the gradations between the extremes. Judgments of quality, indicating your preferences, are not based upon absolute measurements. Rather, they are dependent upon your previously established values, which are based on beliefs of the good and bad from prior experience. Your judgment of financial well–being, for example, is conditioned to levels of income and expenses relative to which you have become accustomed. For instance, I felt quite fortunate as a student whenever I had *any* extra money for entertainment. Your sense of sufficiency and material comfort depend upon these relative expectations.

The judgment of *association* refers to your relationship and identification with an object or a condition, and to your impression of being unified with or separated from it. The statements, *I am an American citizen* or *I am not a watercolor artist*, reflect an association through physical relationships. The combined judgments of quality and association form your self-evaluation from which you build your self-identity. Such evaluations, in turn, affect the judgment of acceptance.

Immanuel Kant, in the *Critique of Pure Reason*, abstracted the content of judgments into four components: quantity, quality, relation, and modality (1990, 54-67). In this book, Kant's components of quantity and quality are combined into a new definition of the term *quality*. A hungry man, for instance, might view one apple as being good and the quantity of two as better in a quality judgment of goodness. Ten apples might result in a bellyache and, thus, are judged as a bad choice with regard to his hunger. Therefore, this synthesis of Kant's components into *quality* involves both subjective and nonlinear factors.

Kant's component of *modality* is combined with *relation* to express physical *association*. The term relation, as used herein, refers to external objects that are, in Kantian terms, *existent*, *probable*, *conditional*, or *hypothetical*. Another type of association is introduced here for non-physical, conscious entities. The resulting judgments of quality and association specifically relate to one's subjective evaluation of experience, both necessary in providing the required concepts to express value judgments and sufficient to convey all such judgments. Judgments formed with the two components, *quality* and *association*, have direct correspondence to emotions, as will be addressed in a later chapter. Kant's four components are more generally applicable to non-subjective categories.

Kant maintains that a consciously aware observer can only be understood as a *subject* and not as an *object*, and that his categories of understanding apply only to the object and *not* to the subject (1990, 214-221). Kant objects to the introduction of metaphysics and maintains that consciousness can be understood only in a transcendental sense, excluding all empirical elements. Certainly there are no empirical elements—the basis of Kant's categories of understanding—in a non-material entity such as a conscious being. Consciousness, itself, is ever changing and elusive and not to be objectified. In accepting the non-material nature of consciousness as transcending time and space, but still immanent through existential experience, a new and appropriate category of association must then be adapted. We exist, yet we must define this existence in new terms.

From a worldly perspective, a person can relate to a physical self-image with material properties. However, as a non-material, conscious being, one can have a spiritual *self-identity* in addition to, but distinct from, the physical self-image. Thereby, *identity* is a category of association applicable to our conscious being in its evaluation of experience. *Identity* is employed as a *non-physical extension* opposite of Kant's relationship category. Such an approach involves recognition of an entity that is *aware of and identifies with* the ability for conscious awareness and subsequent self-reflection, as *I am a being of conscious awareness capable of thinking*. Furthermore, if we assign characteristics and abilities to consciousness, as for example, *freedom in thought*, such secondary properties, as word and concept, can be considered as non-material objects to be contemplated in *association with this* self-identity.

The Human versus Spiritual Self

If an intergalactic being making first contact with earth called me on a videophone and asked who I was, I might respond by describing my physical person: *See, this is my body, I have two hands, each with five fingers. And this is the way I am dressed today, but sometimes I dress more formally. That is my wife over there and that is a picture of our children, a few years younger of course.* I might continue by describing my job, various personal relationships, and how my favorite team is playing. Thus, a large portion of one's human self-image is determined by worldly circumstances, which change throughout our lives. However, through such a material assessment, do we really answer the questions: *Who are we, and what are we?*

Our mental response to every experience makes a statement to the Generative Principle about who we believe ourselves to be. These thoughts that focus on our human situation usually obscure the idea of us as spiritual beings. A more introspective part of us also knows that we are something more than is described as physical experience. We have two perspectives relative to identity with one associated with our physical relationships termed the *Human Self*. This corresponds to what Antonio Damasio terms, the *autobiographical self* (1999, 172-176). The second is associated with our innate being, or *Conscious Self*. Most often, we identify ourselves in a worldly context rather than as a non-physical being. Only during select occasions, as in mindful reflection or meditation, do we consider our self-conscious identity—that is, as an entity *conscious of being conscious.* Yet, it is this latter identity that is critical in finding a personal spirituality. Note that the *same consciousness* is aware of either the *Human Self* or the *Conscious Self*, and requires merely a shift in perspective. Whereas the Conscious Self has a concept of time due to its association with the Human Self, the Human Self is necessarily defined in terms of time and space.

Many worldly judgments regarding the Human Self often become associated with our conscious identity because we do not discriminate between the two. For example, if I make the announcement, "I am a worthy person," I might be referring to a self-judgment that I deserve respect, recognition, or possibly a raise in salary. But, judgments of being a good human being can be internalized, complementing the Conscious Self. For instance, by supporting an orphanage in an underdeveloped country, one could feel, *I am a good person*. Conversely, internalized judgments of Human Self-depreciation can be very harmful to conscious identity.

The subdivision of *association* into physical *relationship* and conscious *identification* is necessary to conceptually distinguish between these two identities. Worldly relations have no effect upon our conscious being unless we internalize a physical condition and incorporate it into our self-image at the *being* level. Importantly, we cannot be alienated from our spiritual nature except by lack of realization and attention. The two options for the association judgment are illustrated in the following figure. We recognize our Human Self through sensory awareness of physical relationships, whereas our Conscious Self is available only through introspective self-identification.

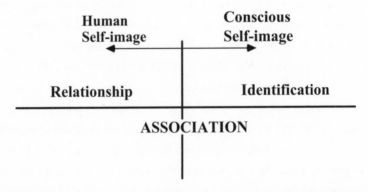

Figure 4. Judgments of Association for the Human and Conscious Self

When judgments of association and quality are combined, as they usually are, we obtain *value judgments*. For example, if you say, "I am a good golfer," you are relating yourself to the image of a golfer having favorable qualities; that is, you *value* your self-image as a good golfer. One's Conscious Self-identity is affected in a positive way with uplifting statements like, *I am a person of worth and integrity*, or in a depreciating manner with a statement such as, *I am a hopeless sinner*.

As human beings, we tend to assess our capabilities and limitations by realizing what we have done, what we can do now, and what we might be able to do in the future. For instance, I can recall my past achievements and current successes, but know that I can never be a trapeze artist and will not win the Nobel Prize in physics. It is important to know and express who we are as unique human beings within our contingencies. In this way we can live our lives with the passion of our convictions, and with authenticity rather than self-deception.

Structure of Conscious Evaluation

Value judgments, as elemental discriminations, form the building blocks in the development of all convictions. The Generative Principle, in turn, transforms convictions into kernels of belief. The two fundamental judgments relative to evaluation, in summary are:

Quality   The article is good or bad.

Association   Conscious Self (we identify with the article), or Human Self (we are related to the article as object).

All of your interactions with the Generative Principle can be reduced to these fundamental judgments of quality and association, in addition to the judgment of acceptance that is addressed separately. Kernels of belief incorporating such judgments are precursors to the formation of physical experience through the Generative Principle, and to associated emotions and their accompanying physiological feelings. These kernels can be considered as personalized mini-archetypes and, as with all archetypes, they tend to manifest themselves.

In Figure 3, the right-hand side represents identifications exclusive to your conscious mind. The left side represents physical relations peculiar to your human experience. In both the conscious and human perspectives, you make subjective quality judgments regarding what *appears* either favorable or unfavorable. This judgment of relative goodness results in the respective divisions between the upper and lower halves of the graph. The graph is, thus, divided into four quadrants representing the States of Conscious Evaluation, whose characteristics are summarized below and described in more detail in later chapters.

The right-hand side represents evaluations of your Conscious Self, or your internal being, without worldly trappings. Your Conscious Self, with self-awareness, is your essential being. The ability to *think* requires freedom to do so, with *freedom* or *free* will identified as an attribute of conscious being. Consciousness attends to thoughts volitionally generated by it, or to experiences presented by the Generative Principle. In thinking, consciousness supplements experience by drawing its language from memory within subconscious mind in terms of words, symbols, and imagery. Conscious control and direction is maintained through discipline and focus. Otherwise, it can be lost through laxity allowing emergence of idle subconscious imagery, such as daydreaming or distraction by worldly events.

Another characteristic of Conscious Self is inherent *goodness*. As an *entity of the present moment*, consciousness is incorruptible, and being of a non-material nature it is unaffected by any prior action or condition of the Human Self. The agency of Consciousness moves in freedom with an absence of external opposition or resistance.

Pictured in the upper right of Figure 5 is the state of *Elevated Consciousness*. The Conscious Self is elevated through realizing and expressing *I am* good, then identifying with goodness at the being level, bringing feelings of joy, satisfaction and fulfillment with an enhanced sense of self-worth. Note that this value judgment of being good involves the very important, first person, present tense statement, I am, which is reminiscent of the great "I am" declaration by divinity in Judeo/Christian/Islamic literature, e.g., "I am that I am." Related phrases are: *I feel appreciated by you, I love you*, or *I feel fulfilled*. It is beneficial to spend a good deal of time in this self-nurturing state of well-being. Dwelling in this state is facilitated through the practice of mindfulness and meditation, as later will be described.

In the lower right of Figure 5, we find the state of *Depressed Consciousness*, which typically incorporates emotions such as unworthiness, deprivation, despair, and depression. Statements identified with non-goodness (*I am not good* or *I am bad*) characterize this conscious position. From this perspective, one tends toward thoughts such as: *There is no use trying any more because I am a failure; I am so bad that no one wants me*; or, *I feel abandoned*. "Non-good" is often associated with anger. Such anger is either directed inward to the Conscious Self, outward toward the world, or both. Dwelling in this state of mind is an unpleasant experience to be avoided if possible. However, we all slip into it on occasion. We will later examine pathways to escape from this state when entrapped within it.

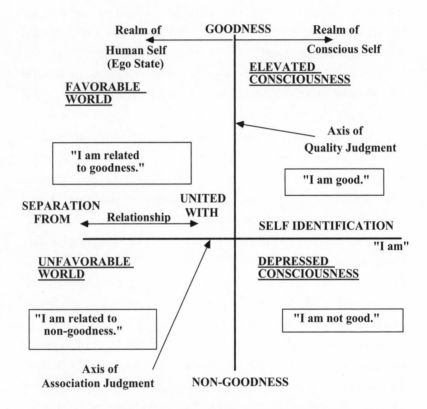

Figure 5. Four States of Conscious Evaluation formed
by the Fundamental Judgments

The realm of the Human Self or Ego State, on the left-hand side of Figure 5, represents your physical identity. Here, you demonstrate activities of consciousness through the avenue of worldly objects and activities. This self-identity has a history, owns possessions, and is anxious about the events of tomorrow. Defined in terms of time and space, this is the self-image presented to others utilizing physical descriptions, relationships, capabilities, and limitations. This physical self represents your temporal being that continually changes over the course of a lifetime.

The distinction between the physical, human person and the formless, conscious counterpart is not intended to demean the physical in any way. The human body does not represent a lower nature, nor should we attempt to transcend it in favor of some ethereal form. Our bodies and their worldly experiences are necessary and important. Although we fundamentally are spiritual beings, we need this phenomenal means of external awareness and personal demonstration as we express ourselves through worldly affairs.

The state of *Favorable World* occurs when you judge your physical experiences as beneficial. Some days everything seems to go your way. The air is fresh and crisp and you feel healthy and invigorated, or you engage in an enjoyable activity while in the company of loving companions. Perhaps, you feel comfortable and secure with adequate compensation, or you just have a creative outlet. Here you effectively declare: *I am related to goodness*, with goodness as a physically accountable quantity. In quantifying this worldly goodness, we typically measure *abundance* by the amount of money in the bank, *harmony* by the health of our human body, *security* by the job in which we work, *happiness* by our intimate relationships, and *satisfaction* by the success of our team. We experientially encounter this type of worldly goodness in everyday events, as well as through imaginative visualization, in the recall of past successes, and even in dreams.

As we assign values of worth and meaning to these physical manifestations of the Favorable World, we also form *attachments* to them. They appear to be the source of our fulfillment and we become dependent upon them, literally counting our blessings in a quantitative way. This process depicts a very reasonable and pragmatic worldly view of *accountable goodness*. Such a viewpoint causes no problems unless we associate self-worth with this mercurial and vulnerable expression of goodness.

In striving to maintain the Favorable World status, we typically remark: *I need an increase in pay to improve my life-style; We have a great relationship, but we must work to sustain it; or, I will feel a lot better if I can lose about ten pounds.* Material goodness is *conditional* upon external circumstances that are often not under our control. Mother Nature—with whom we credit road conditions, the chance of winning the lottery, the outbreak of a strange virus, weather, and all things unpredictable—personifies the outward face of the Generative Principle. Behind the seemingly random variation of events in time and space lie unseen intelligence, order, balance, and purpose that are usually beyond our understanding.

The problem of associating self-worth with material good is that everything physical is transitory, *it comes, it is here, and then it goes*. If our self-image involves a clinging attachment to some material thing, then as it departs, so goes our self-worth. This impermanency of the physical world lies in contrast to the permanency of our conscious being. The Generative Principle, not us, is in command of these manifestations. As long as our human identities are dependent upon experiences in the Favorable World, we are forever possessed with a degree of uncertainty: *Will goodness continue or will it not?* Uncertainty comes hand-in-hand with its sister, the emotion of anxiety, as anxiety is always coupled to worldly attachments. For a stable establishment of self-worth, we need something more reliable than material goodness. Only as we connect with the here-and-now experience, does this uncertainty subside.

The state of an *Unfavorable World* lies at the bottom-left of the graph. Some days everything appears to go wrong: You are running late for an important appointment, the traffic is heavy, and your gas tank is almost empty; an unexpected tax bill due in two weeks leaves you wondering where you will find the money; or, your stomach is still churning over a difficult encounter at work and you fear that an ulcer is developing. The Unfavorable World involves relations with consequential things appearing antagonistic toward your well-being. The objects and events of this state are also fraught with uncertainty and the emotion of anxiety, but can also entail a greater potential for harm than do those of the Favorable World.

During encounters of an Unfavorable World, the judgment of quality is reflected in statements such as: *I am related to non-good; I am threatened and afraid; I made a terrible mistake that I regret; or, I am worried about the outcome of my interview*. An unsatisfactory situation may affect the quality of human experience, but an even greater threat to us occurs when we identify our self-worth with a seemingly bad encounter.

In the Unfavorable World we associate the idea of a threat with an event that causes pain or deprives us of fulfillment and satisfaction. Pain can be either physical or emotional, and either immediate, potential, or a burning ember from the past. What is this quality of non-good or badness to which we refer? Are *good* and *evil* absolute values in the world? Not exactly, for as Emerson expressed it: "Good is positive. Evil is merely privative, not absolute: it is like cold, which is the privation of heat." (Dillaway 1990, 35). In other words, the bad does not actually oppose good, but rather it is the apparent deficiency of it, although in our usual dualistic thinking, the two are represented as being opposite. It is helpful to think of this vertical scale like that of a thermometer showing *degrees* of perceived goodness.

ng an echo from Shakespeare's Hamlet: *There is nothing r bad but thinking makes it so.*

There are experiences that some regard as evil, but this judgment is properly restricted to the material world. There is nothing manifested as inherently good or evil, even though our subjective judgment may label it so. The judgment of non-good, discordance, or evil is an abstraction implicitly meaning the absence or shortage of good. Non-good is, therefore, not an inherent property of the experience itself, but rather a quality judgment regarding it[1].

During experiences of extreme pain that saturate the senses and dominate the function of awareness, the physical existence of non-good seems very *real*, definitely *bad*, or perhaps *evil*. Here, the Generative Principle is knocking urgently at the door[2]. Rather than avoiding Her message, it is far better to experientially accept Her imposition in your awareness. Simply feel the pain, especially the emotions, knowing that the content and meaning of Her message is hidden somewhere within and that the occasion eventually will pass. All things created by the Generative Principle are appropriate and proper, but the Human Self does not always understand its role in this karmic unfolding. Expectations of the ego as to how things should be, rather than how they are, result in the judgment of events being bad, providing a source for human suffering.

Emerging Spiritual Awareness

An early story of conscious discrimination is presented in the Biblical Book of Job of the first millennium BC. In this Semitic culture, the creative powers resided with the male God, Yahweh, who is portrayed as a God of violence and injustice, displaying emotions of rage and jealousy in treatment of his faithful servant,

Job. Carl Jung associates this idea of God with the then-prevailing earlier stage of collective unconscious content of this culture. Job, in contrast to this portrayal of God, demonstrates an unfailing faith in goodness and justice, enduring his miserable fate as a loyal subject of this God.

Job displays the conscious aptitude for discrimination from which justice is derived through a distinction between good and evil. God, on the other hand, exhibits the trait of amorality and indiscriminate punishment. Job realizes the inherent goodness of God through his faith, despite his unjust treatment through opposite manifestations. As Jung expressed it: "Yahweh is not split but is an *antinomy*—a totality of inner opposites"(Jung, 1973, 7).

Our own experience still mirrors a mixture of the good and bad according to the collective and personal content of subconsciousness. We frequently experience our projections as painful situations that appear unjust, and with anguish cry out to the creative powers in the manner of the crucified: "My God, my God, why hast thou forsaken me?" Such recognition of evil is not in vain, for discrimination has an effect upon the subconscious mind and consequent manifestations. As the above exclamation by Jesus is associated with his divine ascension, so does our discrimination and affirmation of goodness provide an uplifting of consciousness that renders a corresponding evolution of subconsciousness.

Allegorically, Job's unshaken belief in God's goodness and justice appears to have had an effect upon God, as he evolved into one of love and fairness as projected by authors of Biblical chapters written after the beginning of the first millennium. Job's protest to God regarding his unjust punishment was not in vain. He exercised the powerful freedom of consciousness, affirming truth *according to his conviction* while facing evidence to the contrary, and, thereby, propounded a quality that *should be* attributed to a God of unimaginable powers. In this respect, Job was a heroic incarnation of a spiritual being.

Both the subconscious mind and the natural world, itself, contain a union of opposites, like Yahweh's antinomy. The powers behind nature's raw manifestations are awe-inspiring and, like Yahweh, they produce experiences that sometimes are unpleasant and seemingly unjust. It is the primary function of conscious discrimination to be aware of, and mentally separate, the relative *good* from the *bad*, and the "with" from the "without."

The evolution of human consciousness is dependent upon the development of such awareness and discrimination. The potential for such activity holds unlimited possibilities for the personal psyche, as well as for improving physical manifestations in the world. It is as if the positive aspects of God, dormant in the collective unconscious, are waiting to be born and to elevate the mind of mankind. Supporting this view are the metaphorical expressions describing the enlightened one, such as finding the Christ within, the Buddha within, the Divine Child, or the Atman.

It is the opportunity and responsibility of each individual

to discover and develop the potential of their

conscious being, ...the Spiritual Self.

Questions for Discussion

(1) What are the three fundamental judgments?

(2) Why is Identity as a subcategory of Association important for recognizing yourself as a conscious being?

(3) What are the two basic perspectives of self-image that we can have for ourselves?

(4) How do we form value judgments? Give several examples. What are the four states of conscious evaluation formed by the fundamental judgments? What state corresponds to how you feel about yourself today?

(5) Why is the Biblical Job described as "a heroic incarnation of a spiritual being"?

Notes

[1]Shunryu Suzuki, giving another perspective for quality evaluation, quoted his Zen master Dogen, "Although everything has a Buddha nature, we love flowers, and we do not care for weeds," and continuing, "This is true of [and characterizes] human nature" (1973, 119).

[2]At this very point in preparing this work, I was stricken with an acute pain in the region of my heart that intensified until I was nearly incapacitated. Although I firmly believed and adamantly stated that it was not a heart attack, I finally yielded to my wife's insistence on calling an ambulance. Emergency room doctors also believed it to be a heart attack and were preparing a potentially dangerous medication until a cardiac specialist eventually declared it to be pericarditis, a viral infection of the heart lining. The pain subsided with proper medication, and following release from the hospital the next day, I added the next paragraph with great humility. A synchronistic directive? Perhaps so.

CHAPTER 5

ENCOUNTERING PROJECTIONS

The Consequence of Hidden Beliefs

Our experiences and self-image change over the course of our lives. As infants, with limited awareness from which to develop a self-image, we came into what appeared to be a very complicated world. Although we do not understand how or why, the Generative Principle had an initial plan for our lives that launched us into the circumstances of childhood. If another spiritual being was born to your parents at the time of your birth, it would not be you. You are a unique individual, a personalized expression of the Generative Principle resulting in a one-of-a-kind you.

As children with limited awareness, we had few options. As our knowledge increased through growth, we were able to exercise more freedom of choice. As adults, we further expand awareness and can realize what complex and wonderful beings we are. Comprehending our interaction with the Generative Principle, learning Her language and realizing the consequence of our own thoughts, all facilitate our process.

Whether we are aware of it or not, we continually communicate with the Generative Principle—*we* in thought and *She* through manifested experiences. Thoughts that we have in the *imagined* privacy of our minds are intimately conveyed to Her as they pass from awareness into subconsciousness. She assimilates this subconscious content, producing dreams, memories, visions, and immediate emotions, in addition to each momentary worldly experience.

We usually do not understand the significance of our own message to the Generative Principle, even though She understands very clearly. For example, when driving in traffic, I am often impatient with slower drivers, especially when they remain in the left lane, *my* passing lane. My impatience and stress convey a belief to the Generative Principle that there is *no extra time*. The Generative Principle responds to this belief by providing me with no extra time, only just enough to complete each task. My schedule always fills the hours of the day. To confirm this, the slow driver appears ahead of me in traffic depleting extra minutes. My recurring thoughts and emotions regarding such situations, assisted by the Generative Principle's compliance, perpetuate this entrapment of urgency. My mental identification with the problem provides for me no passing lane. No one knows us better, and no one is more responsive to us, than the Generative Principle.

However well my life is working, there always seems to be areas of pain and discomfort, where joy, happiness, and fulfillment are not evident. *If I am such a spiritual being*, I ask myself, *why then am I having all of these problems?* I want to know why the Generative Principle is delivering such experiences. Frustrating circumstances can provide us with motivation for discovering our spiritual natures, understanding the Generative Principle, and increasing awareness.

Most of our efforts for dismissing discomfort and increasing satisfaction are superficial endeavors akin to fighting the symptoms of a head cold. We find a remedy to ease the coughing and sneezing, but the virus lives on in our body. In the same way, when we run short of cash we may take out a loan to provide temporary relief, *but the root cause of the situation lives on*. Our meager attempts to combat the symptoms of human inadequacy send signals to the Generative Principle that actually enforce the root idea rather than contradict it.

Life patterns tend to recur like grass perennially appearing in the garden each season. The seeds of these recurring patterns lie deep. But, we can affect their character as we learn to speak effectively to the Generative Principle. To change these root conditions, we need to first comprehend experiences as messages from the Generative Principle. In attempting to correct the maladies of our lives, it is important to note that the *Generative Principle requires no healing*. She is eternally healthy and does Her job quite well. It is a change in the root idea embedded as a kernel within *our subconscious* that will affect our experience.

There are times when we choose *not* to give up our pain. Mental pain and discomfort occur when there is a conflict of values, some of which lie outside our awareness. For instance, I might find myself in an uncomfortable relationship, but I am reluctant to dissolve it because of concern with possible consequences. If there were no conflict involved, selecting an alternative to distress would be simple. These topics of conflicting values will be revisited in later chapters.

> You can, with increasing proficiency, begin to
>
> author the destiny of your life.

The destiny of your life is not so predetermined that you are an eternal pawn of kismet or karma. That which has the appearance of *fate* is merely the apparent trend of the Generative Principle's plan. However, this plan can be altered through your communication with Her. In this text, *karma* in understood to mean the path of one's life determined by both the individual and universal subconscious.

Formation of Your Ego and Shadow

The ancient Greeks offered the injunction of "Know thyself." A wise piece of advice, perhaps, but this is an ever-going process and there is so much that we either do not know or do not recognize. Most colorful aspects of our personalities are formed by two inner-psychic characters known in psychology as *Ego* and *Shadow*, which are formed, respectively, by the fundamental decision of *acceptance* or *rejection*. The material world is the habitat and play-ground of Ego and Shadow. Without them the material world would seem cold, sterile, and meaningless. These two components are often the personification of heroes and villains, appearing either good or evil, for *us* or *against* us.

Your Ego and Shadow are embodiments within the Generative Principle, formed from concepts relating to you that previously were either affirmed or denied and dismissed to your subconscious mind. In addition, underdeveloped aspects, such as your spiritual nature, will at times appear in your personal manifestations. For example, the Generative Principle prompts your consciousness to recall aspects of its own true nature at appropriate occasions through reminders such as a memory, dream, or perhaps the meeting of a kind and caring person.

Your Ego consists of that human self-image which you acknowledge, including all favorably supporting experiences such as your family, job, car, and the clothes you wear. Your Shadow consists of all that you disassociate and negate from your self-image and generally ignore. The Shadow is complimentary to the Ego, with both being active in the formation of your total experience in the physical world.

Generally speaking, your Ego consists of aspects of yourself that you have *accepted* and incorporated into your self-identity. Your Shadow, in contrast, is most likely composed of aspects that were disowned, rejected, or denied. Manifestations of your Ego

and Shadow emerge from your subconscious, affecting your outlook and the nature of your experience. Whereas your Ego is
more available to conscious awareness, your Shadow resides in
subconsciousness where it is more difficult to access.

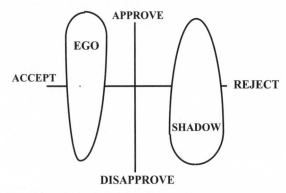

Figure 6. Conscious Decisions Forming the Ego and Shadow

Your Ego can encompass that which is judged desirable, as
well as that which is found offensive. Your Shadow likewise can
extend through both of these evaluations as a counter-supple-
ment to the Ego as illustrated below.

As my Ego encompasses my vocation, I might, for example, find
many aspects of my work rewarding, a Favorable World condition.
Yet, the work also involves schedules and some personal interactions
that I sometimes find stressful, an Unfavorable World experience.
When we honestly acknowledge the world, we find it to be a mixed
bag of both good and bad. The Shadow, of which we have little or no
awareness, pops in unexpectedly to provide many unwanted surprises while still having beneficial, as well as detrimental, aspects.

Your life will be richer and more rewarding as you come to
know both your Ego and Shadow and the habitat of personal values that they embrace. You can begin to know your Ego simply
through self-introspection. You can discern your Shadow, but
only through the more difficult process of accepting and integrat-

ing those manifestations that you find objectionable, offensive, distasteful, or painful. We will later explore several techniques that assist you in this process.

Sometimes we act in a manner that is totally contrary to the self-image that we strive to maintain. We say things that are damaging to relationships, act compulsively to harm our health or finances, or maintain habits contrary to our intentions. These are injections from our Shadow, the dark side of our character, hidden from awareness and unacceptable to our sense of appropriateness. The Shadow appears as a villain or trickster in dreams, as a character that we meet with annoyance, disdain, or embarrassment.

The Shadow's unacceptable character portrays those traits that we do not wish to see in ourselves. By freedom of will, it is possible to circumvent most any human experience through suppression of awareness—but only temporarily, for the Generative Principle is untiringly persistent. Appearances of the Shadow and other unwelcome experiences tend to be repeated in modified form until acknowledged. We unwittingly perpetuate this cycling of undesirable experiences—usually the painful ones—by returning them, again and again, to their subconscious lair through conscious *avoidance mechanisms*.

Two of the avoidance mechanisms that we frequently employ are *rationalization* and *suppression*. Rationalization is the illogical or irrational substitution of an untruth or partial truth for the less desirable whole truth. For instance, if a person does not succeed in obtaining a job that he or she is seeking, the pain of rejection might be avoided by a rationalization such as: *It would not have been good for me anyway*. Or, an individual might avoid taking responsibility for a theft by saying: *I deserve to have the things I want*.

Suppression, on the other hand, is a simple directing of awareness away from that which is less desirable. There are two basic types of suppression. The first type is a normal, practical means of concentrating one's attention in order to focus on an immediate topic of interest. For example, in order to read a book we typically suppress the background sounds of a TV, children playing, or dogs barking—noises not relevant to our immediate priority, but continuing in our low-level awareness. We accept the existence of such undesirable distractions, but in discernment choose to give them no attention. Likewise, when we drive down the road, we are peripherally aware of other cars, but may focus on the conversation we are having with our passenger.

We may shift our awareness to avoid repetitive and annoying occurrences in daily affairs. If a close friend or someone with whom we live has a habit that we do not wish to see, hear or confront, such as smacking lips while eating, we may repeatedly withdraw attention so as to eventually create a *blind spot* where we no longer are aware of the irritation. Now consider a more extreme situation contradicting an egoistic image that is fundamental to self-esteem, or a traumatic event that threatens your concept of an orderly universe. If such an event makes it difficult to operate normally, then we exclude the conditions from our mental imagery and possibly forget their very existence.

This second type of suppression, *extinguishing the undesirable from awareness*, is commonly used by persons so that they can continue to function. For example, a child whose parent abandoned her may be unable to recall the memory because the event resides in the subconscious mind, not easily accessible to consciousness. The conscious act of suppression has been concluded. These painful annihilated events, physical or mental, have detrimental effects upon self-image and, therefore, become an aspect of the Shadow. Many of our human behaviors, appearing inappropriate to the situation and labeled as neurotic, are related to repressed material. An event such as the unresolved death of a loved one, stuffed below awareness to cope with daily activities, might trigger an intense response to another unrelated loss, displaying the repressed emotion. This use of suppression is not uncommon. As some reptiles shed a damaged appendage in order to survive, we avoid memories that tend to be debilitating.

Repressed events, imagery, concepts, or thoughts reside within subconsciousness and are restricted from the normal process of conscious retrieval. Strong denial can become a strongly held conviction, with the decision of non-acceptance resulting in the nonexistence of the object in conscious awareness. Thereafter, awareness is either blind to a manifestation, or else its existence is disowned even though the relationship is evident to others. Fritz Perls terms this nonexistence as *magic annihilation* (1976, 21), where we *abolish in awareness* rather than encounter and challenge the experience. Thus, we employ repression as a means of mental flight from the undesirable instead of confronting it. In an extreme case, this serves as a means of survival. In a milder application, it fabricates an illusionary peace of mind. Repressed content within subconsciousness provides the Generative Principle with material to be re-presented again by means of new experiences. This process, termed *projection*, is discussed in greater detail below. Projection offers our consciousness another opportunity to reprocess and resolve unpleasant events, thereby completing the gestalt.

Denial represents a paradox since the object of denial must exist in order to be disavowed. As an element within the vast body of subconsciousness, the denied object becomes merely one of many possible subjects for the Generative Principle to express. Denial is always an attempt to eliminate that which we feel is not right for us, that which either causes discomfort or is inconsistent with other value judgments. However, the cognizant-dishonesty of denial is an ineffective means to accomplish this goal.

As a case in point, I might deny the fact that I am overeating by rationalizing that I am fatigued and need the food for extra energy; or, someone might deny that their mate has sexually abandoned them because the fact would be devastating to his or her self-esteem. Although denial may be a temporary means for desensitizing and coping, this *quick fix* is always impermanent. Conscious denial of that which exists in awareness is not an act of finality, but rather it represents an *incompletion*. The claim of nonexistence for the undesirable object encountered, either experientially or in imagination, represents an untruth, an imbalance that the nature of things will not accept as a conclusion.

Projection, an Opportunity for Re-Encounter

Projection, in the normal psychological usage originating from Freud, means to attribute to another person or group one's own traits, desires, or emotions that one finds unacceptable in his or her own self. In this connotation, projection is a defensive mechanism employed to avoid objectionable characteristics by ascribing them externally. For example, a person with malicious traits might view the world as being against him.

A broader definition for projection used in this book, and also by Carl Jung, is that projection is a means by which subconscious content is presented again to consciousness. As subconsciousness is here considered as a reservoir within the Generative Principle, then projection is Generative Principle's normal and continual process of manifesting subconscious content. All experience may then be considered as projection—that is, my experience of each person is part of my projection, and vice versa—as if by an entanglement of generative forces.

Projection is the means by which we again meet contents of our subconscious mind, *including* repressed material. Disowned thoughts and feelings are projected forth into new experiences, each in its appropriate time in formations selected by the Generative Principle. Thus, our external experiences provide us with opportunities to confront disowned aspects of ourselves as represented by the Shadow. In other words, the Generative Principle reframes previously avoided material and presents it in the present, as illustrated below.

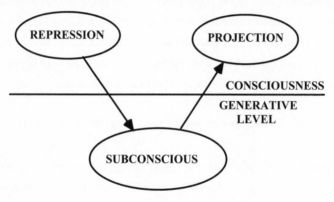

Figure 7. Projection as the Manifestation of Suppressed Material

All worldly experiences are projections of the Generative Principle in response to strongly held beliefs. Of course, favorable experiences manifest from our subconscious content as well as unfavorable ones. For this reason, we will later work with affirmative meditation to facilitate more beneficial manifestations.

Gestalt therapy recognizes the psychic imbalance resulting from unfinished situations and unfelt emotions, and works toward the integration of those missing parts that have been neglected or avoided. The Generative Principle presents these as necessary to complete the whole. The Generative Principle has Her own magical methods. She reaches through and beyond our empty hat—those gaps within our awareness—and pulls out new images from subconsciousness. Acting on embodied beliefs, She redresses the Shadow, generating cyclic physical and mental recurrences similar to those that were denied. This cycle is perpetuated until the rejected thoughts, ideas, and feelings are finally encountered and acknowledged in a truthful reintegration, a completion of the Gestalt. Significantly, as recognized by the Gestalt therapist, *there is always something in the present moment with which to work* so that we never have to attempt that impossible task of reconstructing the past. As beings living only in the present moment, current experiences are always sufficient.

Some people realize, or suspect, that they have had traumatic experiences in the earlier years of their lives, such as physical or sexual abuse. These people often suffer symptoms that suggest the prior occurrence of a trauma. Wishing to eliminate this hidden burden from their lives, they invest a great amount of time and energy, often in therapy, trying to consciously recall the event. Beliefs connected to repressed memories generate new experiences in current awareness through the Generative Principle's process of projection. Such experiences bear relationships to that which was originally denied into repression, but now return to consciousness in a proportion less overwhelming and more manageable. That which we have found painful in the past is presented again, so that sufficient are the problems of today.

When we meet our projected Shadow, we tend to ask: *Why is this person appearing in my life? Why do I deserve this?* If I were to encounter a person who appears abrasive and uncooperative, for example, such an encounter would represent some disposition toward such characteristics within my own subconscious mind. Naturally, I would avoid recognizing the association with my own personality traits because I would find such a Shadow figure unpleasant and offensive. In protecting our self-image, we commonly discount any unfavorable views of ourselves. However, the Generative Principle is efficient and never capricious in Her generation of our experience. All outward experiences are in some way representative and symbolic of something that lies internally.

Material projected by the Generative Principle provides an opportunity for us to reexamine and, eventually, reprocess our beliefs.

Ignoring unpleasant messages and disregarding their meaning will perpetuate the unwanted beliefs. Corrective action begins with attending to the experience, engaging in its objective detail, and acknowledging the accompanying emotions. Through renewed awareness and reevaluation, you may now regain conscious control rather than relinquish it. *Inattention causes a repeat of similar experiences on the treadmill of worldly destiny.* Recognizing the aspects of Ego and Shadow in your projections will assist you in forming a composite picture of your Human Self that is integral to understanding messages from the Generative Principle.

Thus far, we have examined the nature of mind primarily through the cognitive means of ideas and concepts. There is a second level of understanding, equally important, to be addressed next: the level of your heart.

Questions for Discussion

(1) Which of the fundamental conscious decisions is employed in forming the *Ego* and *Shadow*? Give an example of the Shadow.

(2) What is *projection*, and from where does it originate? What information does it use in its formation?

(3) How do you encounter the Shadow in your life?

(4) By what practice can you eliminate your Shadow?

(5) What happens if you ignore your Shadow?

CHAPTER 6

THE HEART CONNECTION

Savoring the Moment

Have you ever eaten an apple? Of course you have! But, have you *fully* experienced it? Have you given it your complete attention, felt with pleasure the crunch between your teeth and the juices flowing around your tongue, tasted the mixed flavors of sweetness and tartness, and noticed the distinct smell in your nostrils? Have you looked at the esthetics of its familiar curves, contrasted by the cavity formed by your bite, and observed its color and firmness in your hand?

It is not easy for us to maintain a focus on what's happening in our physical world without allowing ourselves to be sidetracked. Through the freedom of conscious mind we are aware of many options. Because we have choice as to the use of our conscious mind, we tend to become distracted and wander from the present moment. It might motivate us to give attention to the present moment if we realized that *this immediate experience is especially designed for us and, therefore, is very important.*

Our physical sensations are but one mode of conscious awareness. We most often avoid our physical experience through the mode of thinking, the sacred cow of Western culture. *Think! Think! Think!* is the drumbeat of our society. When we do give attention to the apple, we most likely *think* about it: *Is it soft enough or too green? Do I prefer the Golden Delicious or Granny Smith variety? How much fruit will I have in my diet today?* We categorize, judge, and obtain a lot of facts, but we often miss the passion of the experience in the process.

ly create new experiences through the *process of* ning substitutions for experience at hand: On a .... business trip, I visualize myself back in the comfort of my own home; A politician, after being soundly defeated in a public debate, reflects upon what he could have said to his opponent to change the outcome; A disenchanted lover substitutes partners in the images of her mind. In each case, when we mentally transport ourselves to another time or place, we miss the message of the moment. Visualizations do have their purpose and their own message, but they are often used as means for avoiding less welcomed manifestations from the Generative Principle.

When we do think, we can choose to focus upon the current situation rather than an imaginary diversion. For example, on the business trip, I might well-examine and acknowledge the depths of my stress, fatigue and, perhaps, frustrations, and question if this experience is representative of the way in which I wish to conduct my life. I might even question whether I wish to continue the business at all. The politician, rather than reliving what could have been, could face his humbling experience and reexamine his philosophy. And, the lover could look honestly at her current affair: *Is there meaning and beauty that I have discounted? Do I really wish to leave this relationship and seek another?*

By thinking, we are no longer in contact with the actual physical object, but rather a non-physical abstraction of it. Thinking beyond the current situation can be detrimental to fully experiencing and expressing life. Missing is a deeper engagement through emotions, feelings, and passions. Emotions are not opposed to rationality since they incorporate underlying reasons by way of value judgments. They also provide another means of experiencing and expressing. And, most importantly, emotions assist us in the rational formation of value judgments according to what feels good and bad.

Language of the Heart—Emotion, Feelings, and Passions

To fully *live* an experience involves taking note of emotions as they occur. Emotions have a very special language of their own and are particularly useful in communication with the Generative Principle. To express with emotion is to *speak from the heart*. In addition to being spiritual entities in consciousness, we are also bodies of the phenomenal world with feelings, a part of biological nature. Here, emotions of the mind combine with physiological urges, drives, and instincts to form *passions* signifying meaning and essence that provide another way to engage life.

Since the time of the Greeks there has been continual disagreement among philosophers, and later psychologists, about the meaning of emotions and feelings with no universal consensus of definition. James Hillman, for example, produced a very comprehensive survey on the differing concepts of emotions in his book entitled *Emotion* (1960). It is important to separate the cognitive and material components associated with emotions and feelings. For clarity, two components are identified that operate in conjunction with one another. Emotions, as distinguished in this book, occur as phenomena of consciousness, whereas feelings are experienced in human physiology[1]. Although we may, at times, be more mindful of one component rather than the other, either can alert us to an underlying message of the Generative Principle. Both immediate and reflective types of emotions have their origin in the Generative Principle and are closely linked with feelings. Along with sensory impressions, our awareness of feelings apparently requires brain activity according to the research described by Daniel Goldman (1995, 14-29) and in the extensive work of Antonio Damasio (1999).

Emotions provide us both the vitality and significance of life. Imagery and ideas without emotion would be dull and boring. While emotions are expressively human, imagery and ideas can be documented within the pages of a book or computer memory. You can acquire a greater awareness of emotions and feelings by simply directing your attention toward these functions. Ask yourself: *How do I feel about this?* Then observe the answer in both your mind and body. If the emotion is not readily apparent to the mind, feel the physical sensations. Are your muscles tense? What is the feeling in your abdomen, throat, shoulders, or head? After some practice you can readily identify emotions or feelings as they occur. Such awareness contributes to greater vibrancy in your experience.

Emotions are useful in listening to messages from the Generative Principle, and also in responding to Her, because they serve as unique linkages between consciousness and experience. Your emotions, as we will determine, are efficient indicators of value judgments and, as such, are indicative of underlying thought patterns. Many of us have been taught to ignore or suppress feelings for various reasons. Some dismiss emotions as irrational or useless functions of the mind. Far from being irrational, however, emotions can be related to rational thoughts, as will be described in subsequent chapters. Because emotions have physical components by way of associated feelings as well as cognitive ones, they are dually accessible to awareness.

Existentialist philosopher, Jean-Paul Sartre, described emotions as *phenomena of belief* (1993, 74), and it is maintained here that belief embodies our message within the Generative Principle. Sartre, being a novelist and playwright, as well as philosopher, was an astute observer of human thoughts, emotions, and behavior. In his book, *The Emotions*, he identified two types of emotions, termed *unreflected* and *reflected*. For Sartre, an unreflective emotion occurs concurrent with an encountered experience without prior conscious evaluation, whereas a reflective emotion results from cognitive judgment. This two-fold occurrence has added to the confusion of explaining emotions since some investigators recognize only one of the two, either discounting or totally disregarding the other. According to Sartre, emotion is a *consciousness of the world* (1993, 51), which is another way in which the Generative Principle reveals the world to us. From his neurological perspective, Damasio also identified these two types of emotions (1999, 56).

Many psychologists, in contrast to Sartre's position, believe that thoughts occur immediately following every stimulus or perception, generating the *immediate emotion*. Whether or not preceded by thought, this primary emotional response will be termed the immediate emotion. This primary emotion can occur as a result of either sensory perception of the world, recollection, imagination, or through a dream. If my car suddenly skids on an icy road, I automatically respond with alarm and, perhaps, fear. This immediate emotional response occurs promptly, and sometimes accompanied by automatic behavioral reactions that are seemingly instinctual, prior to *extensive* willful cognitive reflection.

Although we speak of the immediate emotions, they also may be continuous presentations from the subconscious mind rather than being spontaneous with a new experience. Some believe that such emotions can become *hard-wired* in the neurological system of the brain. In other words, we may have lingering thought judgments that persist throughout daily experience forming emotions such as fear, depression, anxiety, anger, or some form of love. Robert Solomon states: "Thus I will insist that emotions are processes, which by their very nature take time and may indeed go on and on. They are not necessarily conscious," (2007, 6). However, what has been wired can be rewired, and subconscious content can be changed by procedures later discussed, thereby terminating the continuing immediacy of unwanted emotions.

The immediate emotion accompanying new experience occurs in *sympathy* with the event, rather than following extensive reflection or conscious deliberation. This primary emotional response and physiological behavior is subjective, sometimes reactionary, and may appear unrelated to an actual physical event. For example, a former combat soldier with Post-Traumatic Stress Disorder might react to the noise of a firecracker as if it were a gunshot, and fear for self-preservation with behavior toward either fight or flight. For any physical event, there may be important psychic events, i.e., *what it reminds one of*. Both perceptions, whether physical or imagined, are products of the Generative Principle and are subjectively interpreted by each person.

Note that it is maintained here that the Generative Principle is the source of *all* experience impinging upon our awareness. This includes some automatic physiological responses programmed within our body, and especially including our brain. During the process of thinking we draw forth from our memory, which lies within the subconscious mind under control of the Generative Principle. We *voluntarily* retrieve content such as words and imagery, and *involuntarily* elicit emotions and some behavioral responses.

The immediate emotion is, therefore, a direct way in which the Generative Principle communicates meaning and significance to our consciousness that is appropriate for our attention. The significance of any thing, event, or circumstance is through emotional awareness of it. Emotion is a language we all intuitively understand with no intellectual interpretation required. For each emotion there is an underlying, *implicit cognitive value judgment*, with an inner meaning that is not always obvious. Recognizing this direct relationship between each emotion and its corresponding value judgment facilitates meaningful dialogues with the Generative Principle.

We evoke the second type of emotional response as we reflect upon and willfully contemplate the world, forming an evaluation of it. For example, I might think: *That undertaking will bring me a lot of personal satisfaction*, whereby I respond with emotional *excitement*. I could further consider: *But I might fail and be severely criticized*, and then be gripped by *fear*. Through contemplation, we can change our evaluation of a mental experience. Note that in order to contemplate anything, we form some sort of abstracted image or idea of it, inevitably colored by the filters of our belief system. In this process of abstraction, the thing or event is no longer an external object of perception. Instead, it is a mental representation through the language of our culture.

Another distinction between the first and second types of emotion is that the first is related to a primary sensation or perception, whereas the second is in response to, and conditioned by, abstract thought. Emotions of the second type, then, depend upon *reflective* value judgments. Emotions have their messages, but they may also to be appreciated as an integral part of the experience, as the *vibrancy* of life. Taking Sartre's position that emotions are coexistent with some experience, either mental or sensory, the second type of emotion is the Generative Principle's immediate reply to each secondary value judgment in forming a mental representation and evaluation of an experience. In consciousness we *indirectly author* those emotions that naturally arise, but it is the Generative Principle who delivers them to us along with ever-changing experience.

Feelings, the physiological analog to emotions, are the Generative Principle's manifestation of emotions in the physical world. Although some consider emotion only as the awareness of physical sensation, this is obviously an inadequate explanation. Correlation does exist between feelings and emotions, but feelings can be ambiguous in the identification of emotions. Both anger and fear, for example, can cause a tightening of the abdomen and a shortness of breath. It is therefore more insightful to look within your heart to understand what emotions are occurring.

Feelings do, at times, flag emotional behavior of which we might not otherwise be aware. During a critical business meeting, for example, I may think of myself as being calm and composed, but then feel a trickle of perspiration run from my armpit down my side, indicating to me that I am anxious. As emotions and feelings are essentially different counterparts of the same manifestation, an awareness of both provides an integration of mind and body. The added dimension of each component increases the depth of experience and further enriches life.

Beliefs within subconsciousness change only as a consequence of new value judgments, while the intensity of accompanying emotion and feelings serve as an indicator of *conviction* in these judgments. As conviction represents the conscious precursor for belief, the emotional import of judgments is significant. Although we spoke previously of the *immediate* and *reflected* emotional components within consciousness, these are abstract constructions for conceptual purposes. In daily activities, our perception, thought, and emotion merge into one continuous and progressive flow of conscious life, with immediate and reflected emotions occurring with little distinction.

Furthermore, the Generative Principle may not instantaneously respond with physical manifestation to your new beliefs, yet you can always reap the emotional experience corresponding with your immediate value judgments. This emotional response, which you experience in forming new, constructive value judgments, can substantiate the *faith* in forthcoming experience, the "substance of things unseen." According to the Generative Principle's infinite judgment, manifestations may be delayed and presented in an unexpected form.

Emotion always has a cognitive forerunner in the form of a value judgment, either by a new conscious evaluation or embodied within a prior subconscious belief. A person is joyful *about* something or fearful *of* something because emotion is in every case based upon an implicit *association* that is a component of the evaluation. Reflective emotions are typically based upon evaluation of objective circumstances, such as, *I am sad because my friend is moving away and I feel a loss.* Emotion is a form of personal expressiveness, i.e., I experience a sadness that is exclusively mine. There is no fixed intellectual interpretation of a material situation without personal value judgment and corresponding emotion.

An object of attention, as a projection from the Generative Principle specialized for each individual, may be shared with other people who may experience entirely different emotions. They will experience their own distinct messages since immediate emotions are personalized. You can never know the emotions of another, nor can they know yours, even if you share the same situations. All emotions are internal and subjective. The objects of experience resonate with kernels of belief within the Generative Principle and are charged with prior value judgments.

Every immediate emotion, feeling, and object of attention present in experience is integral to the composite message from the Generative Principle, and refers to some *personal* antecedent from individual subconsciousness as the causative source. The Generative Principle empowers beliefs to be expressed with the necessary form and energy to produce appropriate manifestations. If we could examine a belief, then we might gain insight into the manifestations of life. But, it is impossible to directly observe the contents of the Generative Principle. You can, however, develop the necessary skills to understand the Generative Principle's personal messages to you and, through your communication with Her, begin to alter your beliefs.

Discovering Kernels of Belief

There is a direct correspondence between emotion and its underlying cognitive significance, for as Sartre observed: "Thus, an overwhelming and definitive quality of the thing appears to us through emotion," (1993, 80). Emotions thereby incorporate the same parameters as the fundamental value judgments and, thus, serve as their indicators. Utilizing this correspondence between thought and emotion, we can transform each emotion into its *cognitive equivalent*. Whereas emotions "just are," the cognitive equivalent derived from emotion is subject to our willful, rational evaluation *and amendment*.

> The revision of the cognitive equivalent
>
> is necessary in reprocessing beliefs.

While immediate emotions from the Generative Principle may descend upon us like "demons from the night," thoughts underlying them contain value judgments subject to our volitional modification as we become aware of them. Determining the cognitive equivalents of emotions is an important step toward revealing the messages of the Generative Principle so that we may exercise our role in the creative process. This does not involve a complicated analysis, but rather a simple transformation from emotion to value judgment using the structure of conscious evaluation.

Hermann Hess, in his novel *Siddhartha*, describes a man on his personal spiritual journey. Having left Gotama, the Buddha or Perfected One, Siddhartha paused and pondered his feeling about separating himself from the great teacher: "He pondered deeply, sinking down into the depths of this feeling as through deep water, until he reached a point where the causes lie—for to know the causes, so it seemed to him, that is what thinking is, and only in this way do feelings become knowledge instead of being wasted; in this way they become meaningful and begin to radiate what is within them" (Hess, 2000, 30). Learning to understand the causes underlying emotions and feelings is to listen to the messages of the Generative Principle.

The lore of the metaphysician is that *fear attracts the object of fear into experience.* The underlying foundation of this folk wisdom is that fear has the cognitive equivalent of a *threat is approaching me.* This evaluation accompanying fear, held with conviction until it is embodied as a subconscious kernel, can indeed manifest into a threat, thereby demonstrating the emotion to be self-fulfilling. Fortunately, this process applies to positive emotions as well. Thus, emotions provide the psychic energization of ideas.

Experiences appearing to repeat themselves result from the same kernel of belief incorporating value judgments indicated by immediate emotions. The perceived experience connects with a corresponding archetypal kernel resulting in a psychic resonance that produces an indicative emotion. It is as if an alchemical process transmutes those value judgments into emotions and physiological expressions. The cognitive equivalent, as the underlying *significance* of an experience and its root cause, can be inferred from the immediate emotion and examined in the light of consciousness. A determination of the cognitive equivalent reveals the value judgment that is the counterpart of the subconscious kernel, the latter forever remaining in the obscurity of the Generative Principle.

Immediate emotions occur directly with or following the experience, but we feel a subsequent emotion in reevaluating the experience. If this secondary, reflective emotion coincides with the original immediate emotion, then we are dwelling upon the same value judgment of the kernel. We perpetuate and enforce the occurrence of similar experiences by leaving the kernel unchanged through repeti-

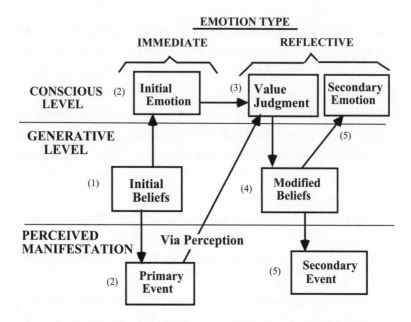

Figure 8. Emotions Relative to the Immediate and Reflective Conditions

tive value judgments and corresponding emotions. The following illustration exemplifies how forming a different value judgment modifies the belief, resulting in a new experience.

If I encounter a seemingly bad situation and initially respond with anger, for example, the cognitive equivalent remains unaltered as long as this primary emotion is maintained. Anger, coupled with aggressive action, may indeed be appropriate, especially if it leads to a constructive change. But as shown in the above illustration, if I reevaluate the situation, the original cognitive equivalent is altered, thereby building a kernel of belief for a new experience.

Do all thoughts lead to beliefs? Thoughts incorporating value judgments tend to form kernels according to the intensity of conviction. The more clear and unobstructed your value judgment, the greater your conviction becomes. Ambiguity and indecisiveness dilutes conviction, reducing the effectiveness of altering beliefs. Beliefs that are inconsistent, or even contradictory with one another, may exist simultaneously within subconsciousness. Manifestations of such opposing values cause many of the tensions within our lives, resulting in occasions of confusion and even chaos. Furthermore, although convictions contradicting laws of nature do not result in physical manifestations, they may find phenomenological expression in the mind of the believer, as in psychotic aberrations.

Emotions arising from current thoughts provide immediate feedback revealing how we *feel about a thing*, contrasting to *what we think about it*. Emotional feelings have been termed a "sixth sense," providing an interpretive dimension that augments the more factual information obtained from the five sensual feelings. Your belief system is quite complex, with many interrelationships. We often mix such emotional considerations with rational thinking, such as, *I am aware of the stress in my job, but I feel that the rewards will be worth it*. If the stress in your job begins to cause a stomach ulcer, are you willing to accept the consequences of altering your work patterns and risk the loss of anticipated rewards? To what extent do you think that rewards contribute to your sense of self-worth and happiness? Do you consider your health to be expendable in pursuit of your goals, or is your body a sacred vehicle of human existence? By identifying value judgments in your dialogue with the Generative Principle, you will attain insight into the nature of your beliefs and avoid unpleasant experiences. There is *no external authority* to determine values for your life. Rather, it is your creative privilege.

When conflicts occur, they present an opportunity

to reexamine underlying values. Therein lies the utility

of value judgments, cogitative equivalents,

and the kernels of belief.

Fundamental Emotions

Emotions have a direct, conditional association with thoughts, overlaying corresponding cognitive relationships identified with the four States of Conceptual Evaluation. These emotions provide our two-dimensional structure of value judgments with a third dimension. Through the symbols of language, concepts may be communicated to others with reasonable accuracy, yet emotions remain subjective. Although emotions, too, have their names, each person may know them differently.

Emotions are consistently expressive of the two fundamental value judgments of quality and association. Nathaniel Branden (1971, 76) arrived at this relationship, explaining it as follows: "Implicit in every emotional response is a *dual* value judgment ...Every emotion reflects the judgment 'for me' or 'against me' and also 'to what extent.' Strictly speaking, these are not two separate value judgments, they are integral aspects of the same value judgment; they may be separated only by a process of abstraction." Thus, the abstractions of quality and association, necessary to provide structure for conscious evaluation, also provide the basis for emotions. *Joy* and *anger* constitute two fundamental extremes of the emotional spectrum and, respectively, are associated with the experiential qualities evaluated as goodness and non-goodness, favorable and unfavorable, or in Branden's terms, "for me" and "against me."

As the most primitive of emotions, they are readily observable in infants who associate joy with gratification and fulfillment of needs, and anger with frustration and deprival. Infants make little distinction between the object of their attention and themselves as the subject. Their discrimination of associations is largely undeveloped since their contact boundaries have not yet evolved. For infants, gratification or frustration is linked with a tenuous perception of goodness. The infant identifies an object of attention, such as food, warmth, or comfort, and then responds to its availability or deficiency; smiling at the sight of the milk bottle or crying when it is removed, with joy or anger following as corresponding fundamental emotions. As we grow older, experience expands the range of awareness, allowing us increasingly finer distinctions between objects of attention and ourselves, with emotions becoming more complex. The fundamental emotions of joy and anger become components within other emotions. For example, hope includes latent joy, whereas fear entails a component of anger.

The judgment of association is divided into two parts, corresponding to the Human Self and the Conscious Self. Associations in the material world of the Human Self are termed *relationships*. These physical relationships always entail a degree of *separation*, as discussed below. The judgment of separation for the Conscious Self in the non-material realm involves degrees of identification with aspects of one's spiritual nature (conscious freedom, goodness, etc.). A second pair of fundamental emotions, corresponding to the polar opposites of physical separation and spiritual identification is *anxiety* and *peace*.

External, physical objects always have some degree of separation from us, either existing or potential. Therefore, there is always a degree of *uncertainty* in their meaning and worth. Objective evaluation involving uncertainty inevitably produces some anxiety at the emotional level, anxiety being fundamental to the human, materially manifested condition. In other words, a degree of anxiety is unavoidable except when we attend to the comfort and security of our inner being.

Your Conscious Self is independent of worldly *uncertainties* and is, thus, free from anxiety and open to peace. But, this type of freedom is realized only when you turn attention inward and find peace as an attribute of your conscious being. Whereas a multiplicity of unforeseen worldly events is encountered each day, your internal nature is unchanging and always available. The eternal quality of your true self is consistent and immutable like a rock. This inalterable nature, independent of human feelings or self-image, is an available option of awareness. Carl Jung speaks of a *stone* as being an archetypal symbol of the Self, with Self as the whole being (Jung 1964, 206-210).

> In the quiet acceptance of your conscious freedom,
>
> in contrast to the conditional, phenomenal world,
>
> you will encounter the emotion of peace.

All emotions encountered within your Spiritual Self include components of peace and joy. In the human, material condition, one may find a *relative peace* in the absence of conflict, yet an inevitable uncertainty of the future persists along with associated anxiety.

Value judgments underlie the occurrence of all emotions. The identification of value judgments corresponding to arising emotions furnishes the most expedient procedure for understanding messages of the Generative Principle. The method for this determination is simply that of introspection, made easier by organizing both emotions and value judgments within the Four States of Conscious Evaluation as shown in the following illustration.

The State of Elevated Consciousness involves a self-evaluation of goodness and a self-identification with a being having freedom in consciousness. Peace, love, and joy are characteristic emotions of this state. Proceeding counterclockwise, the Favorable World is a human identity having relationships with material experiences that can provide, under various conditions,

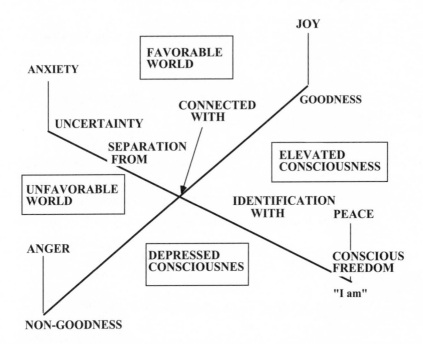

Figure 9. Fundamental Emotions and Corresponding Thought Judgments.

emotions such as happiness, hope, or calmness. The Unfavorable World also involves a human identity, but one having unfavorable experiences involving such emotions as anger, fear, or anxiety. The State of Depressed Consciousness entails a self-evaluation of non-good with self-depreciation. Typical emotions are depression, hopelessness, shame, anguish, and anger.

We first examine emotions inherent to the state of Elevated Consciousness, and then proceed counterclockwise through the remaining states in the following chapters. Human values are very complex and, likewise, are personal emotions. The graphical illustrations that follow provide a first-order understanding of emotions and their relationships to subjective thought judgments.

Questions for Discussion

(1) As defined in this book, what distinction is made between emotions and feelings?

(2) What is the value of emotion in communicating with the Generative Principle?

(3) What are cognitive equivalents?

(4) What is the significance of experiences that tend to repeat themselves in a similar manner?

(5) How do thoughts generate beliefs?

(6) Why is some degree of anxiety often encountered in identity with the Human Self?

(7) What fundamental emotions are encountered in identity with your Spiritual Self?

Notes

[1] Robert Solomon gave a lucid discussion of the distinction between emotion and feeling in his essay *Emotions and Choice* (1980).

CHAPTER 7

THE ENTITY OF YOUR CONSCIOUS MIND

The Nature of Your Divinity

Metaphorically speaking, your consciousness is the *masculine* God actualized in your unique incarnation. Yet, what conscious attributes warrant such a divine identity? How can you accept such character not evidenced by worldly circumstances, and incorporate this identity so that it can be beneficially employed in everyday practical living in this phenomenal world? All great things appear quite simple once they are understood. So it is with your spiritual nature, which is to be discovered through quiet, introspective observation.

A shift in perspective is necessary in order to encounter this divinity within. The first step is to accept the possibility that there is more to you than meets the eye, and that your prior history and opinions of society do not affect your true nature. Your inner reality is not determined by popular consensus, no matter how much conviction lies behind it. Spiritual identity can be adopted without any inflation of the human ego. On the contrary, identity with ego is more likely to be *lessened*. (A god without an ego?) Consider, for example, the humility of the Buddha and Christ.

Looking back at the history of science, there was a time during our most recent millennium when all learned scholars taught that the sun revolved around the earth. This proclamation seemed obvious enough as one simply observed the sky. When we consider how views radically changed during the past millennium, we realize that they will continue to change. Science never reaches a plateau. So-called *facts* that now go unquestioned will later be recalled with a headshake and smile. It is likely that our concept of personal identity will evolve in a similar manner.

Many medical scientists still maintain, in an inversion of cause and effect, that functions of your mind are solely determined by your brain and nervous system. This is a reasonable assumption if the point of reference includes only observable phenomena of the body, analogous to watching the sun apparently revolving around a viewer on the earth. But, the Generative Principle provides you with a body that is a suitable vehicle to operate in this complex worldly environment—with conscious activity reflected therein. Identity solely with the body is a difficult mask to see beyond. But, it is important for you to realize that you enjoy a consciousness that is free to create its own mental pathway.

You may drive a car and identify with its model, style, color, running condition, and road performance. Yet, you are not a car. Likewise, you are not just the human body that transports you during this incarnation, even though you have a considerable investment in your physical circumstance, an identity enforced by society. By releasing this image, if only for brief periods of time, you can realize the greater realm of divine self-reality.

Be very patient with yourself as you venture into meditation and contemplation of your spiritual identity since you have spent many years building upon your human image. Fortunately, it will not take so long to discover the inner world of consciousness. Each glimpse of your eternal reality will be confirmed by intuitive understanding, as well as through the comfort of your emotional and feeling nature.

The following discussion will preview that reality which you will later experience in the quiet solitude of meditation. It is not sufficient to merely intellectually understand your spiritual nature. You must *live it* through inner experience. As no one has learned to fly an airplane by reading manuals, so you must practice the dynamisms of your spirituality within the realm in which it exists. The fruits of consciousness that nourish you along the way are joy, thanksgiving, love, and peace. Qualities of your Spiritual Self are independent of your human circumstances. Although you may comprehend these qualities—finding that they correlate with many ideas from sacred literature found about the world—these ideas will have no personal meaning for you until you encounter them in the solitude of your own consciousness.

A great misconception about being spiritual is that one needs to be pious and reserved. This belief inhibits the vibrancy of life, itself. Your spirituality offers a joyful freedom of expression in the world ranging from the exuberance of creativity, through the fulfillment of relationships, to a quiet serenity of time spent alone. To *follow your bliss*, as Joseph Campbell so implored us, is to find your personal spiritual path, for they are one and the same. Realize the goodness of your life, knowing and feeling the *harmony and ecstasy* of living as the passion of your Spiritual Self.

During times of quiet, personal meditation, reflect upon the nature and qualities of your conscious being. This approach, successfully pursued by millions of seekers throughout the millennia, produces a remarkable increase in the inner quality of your life. As you read, understand, and patiently seek inner confirmation, the Generative Principle responds by substantiating these qualities within your experience.

Your Eternal Being

The Generative Principle creates all things physical—or at least presents the illusion of such to our awareness—including the space, time, and substance characterizing human experience. Yet, your nonphysical, conscious being is in a domain separate from all physical objects including your human body. Your spiritual nature is permanent, independent of time and space extensions. With only thoughts and emotions changing, your spiritual nature provides you with a stationary perspective from which you survey unfolding events. Each consciousness is a singularity in the apparent flow of time, likened to a rock fixed in the current of a stream. In consciousness, you exist only in this instant of *now* which has neither past nor future, but which is eternally present, unconditioned by worldly circumstances.

Momentary living clears a path for joy. When you realize that your consciousness exists only in this instant of now and that you are born fresh each moment, you will encounter the world with a sense of discovery. You are unbound from the past and future as you focus upon the experience before you. Thus, you are liberated from anxiety, hopes, and regrets. *Forever* is a concept of time, but as Paul Tillich in The *Eternal Now* points out: "[T]he eternal stands above the past and present" (1963, 125). He further states: "It is the eternal 'now' which provides for us [humans] a temporal 'now'" (1963, 131). You are eternal as a spiritual being, but are aware of time as a human being. There is an internal you, the real and natural you, that is changeless. As a spiritual being, you exist in an eternal reality that is beyond the ephemeral reality of your human experience. Although your human circumstances do not affect this eternal you, they may affect *who you think you are.*

The idea of being eternal is initially difficult to comprehend. You may ask: *Where did I come from? When did I begin?* But, these questions are of little relevance for an eternal being. Yet, *Who am I?* still remains a legitimate and most important question. You have a double identity in your human form. Therefore, you may ask: *Does my life on this earth have a purpose? What is the relationship between my life and that of other persons?* The fact that you are eternal does not imply that you are static or invariable. On the contrary, it is your nature to continually move, change, and creatively express as a human. Your freedom of will makes your life unique among all others. You are an individual expression and there will never be another like you. The manifestations of your beliefs through the Generative Principle are likewise distinctive. In this way, your visions of the world are unparalleled. As people strive to preserve various species of plants and animals from becoming extinct, how much more valuable are you as a one-of-a-kind, self-conscious entity?

Your conscious being exists singularly in the eternal now. Any reference to yourself in this context is properly done in the first person, present tense as, "I am ...". At the being level, you are. In affirming your spiritual identity, it is important to use these "I am..." statements. Although your Spiritual Self is eternal, you may not realize or benefit from its divine attributes until you *accept* and *declare* this identity within your own conscious. Your self-declaration, even in the form of thought, is a powerful determinant in communicating with the Generative Principle. As an example, you might affirm:

I am a unique representative of the life force, knowing and expressing itself in human experience. I exist in this eternal now and remain unchanged in my nature as I observe this parade of events in my awareness. I accept this life I live, and acknowledge the inherent goodness that is mine, now, in eternity.

Your Unbounded Freedom and Goodness

Freedom occurs as you express the nature of your eternal spiritual being that is beyond any external conditioning. Freedom in consciousness is your ability to select and evaluate the contents of your awareness, and is conditioned only by the knowledge of your choices and the values you have adopted. You inevitably make evaluations regarding everything coming into your awareness and, in this way, accumulate a set of values. As similar experiences occur, you have some conditioned responses. But, you always have a new opportunity either to accept old values unchallenged or to make new assessments.

For example, if I am having dinner in the home of a foreign host, I might be offered a steaming dish covered with a pastry shell, piping with the aroma of exotic spices. I may be reminded of a previous dish that I disliked and politely decline, or I can choose to respond with the excitement of challenge for a new gastronomic adventure. We never know what lies under the shell! Likewise, the great depth of your Spiritual Self lies partially concealed beneath the covering of your worldly identity and conditioning.

You can grow by expanding your awareness, removing your mental reservations and inhibitions and, thereby, unbinding your conscious freedom. You, in your will to choose, are singular, autonomous, and unfettered—the *exclusive operator* making your decisions. As a conscious being, a most precious capability is your freedom of thought, which means that you can think anything you want. This freedom is a most sacred aspect of your individuality. It provides you with the volition necessary for your role in the sacred marriage with the Generative Principle. It is you, and not She, who possess this conscious autonomy. You, as the masculine component of divinity, are an indispensable element in the creative process.

Conscious freedom knows no opposition. As Sartre remarked: "There is no inertia in consciousness," (1956, 61)[1]. You are not required to make any changes because it is fine to be just the way you are if that is your wish. Your freedom of will is foremost and allows for possibilities and choices. However, along with freedom comes an *existential responsibility*, not only for the decisions and choices you make but for those you don't make.

There is nothing in the realm of consciousness to condemn you, but yourself. Therefore, if you think poorly of yourself, you adopt a misrepresentation. Accepting an unfavorable judgment does not affect the *real* you, though it will certainly affect your outlook and experiences. Self-affirmation is the *correct idea* and, therefore, at the being level *self-negation is an absolute falsehood*. Yet, this truth will not predominate in your experience until it is recognized and adopted. Reflect upon yourself as a conscious entity, stating an affirmation such as the following in the privacy of your mind:

> *I appreciate this freedom in thought that defines this life I live, and I cherish this time of reflection. I accept this occasion to choose how I wish to think of myself, releasing the old, painful images I have adopted. I claim goodness for my inner being and explore what possibilities this offers to my life. I open myself to new opportunities as a result of this decision.*

Self-affirmation requires concentration and attention that becomes increasingly easier with practice. Step-by-step, you can build a stairway toward a higher realization of your own goodness and self-worth and be assured that the Generative Principle will begin Her part in providing corresponding manifestations.

Peace occurs as you recognize and attend to your conscious freedom and inner goodness as being independent of worldly fluctuations. This peace is free of human tension and conflict and is beyond worldly understanding. It is an *internal orientation* recognizing the inalterable nature of conscious life. Nothing from the external, physical world perturbs this inner stillness and balance, unless allowed. Such peace is an emotion of the Conscious Self resulting from an equanimous outlook, with any external tensions balanced in suspension. This equanimity is possible through identification with the unconditioned and uncontested Spiritual Self. Inner peace manifests outwardly into the physical realm as the feeling of patience. This brings composure and tolerance, excludes agitation and resistance, and conveys a general feeling of well-being.

In contrast, peace in the phenomenal world normally is recognized as the absence of conflict. Yet, such temporal conditions entail a degree of anxiety related to maintaining this status. The Human Self can also realize this peace by turning inward during chaotic times, reflecting upon an innate spiritual identity, and finding the goodness of inner life to be substantial, absolute, and beyond external fluctuations. A feeling of peace in the presence of worldly conflict is not illogical. Rather, it provides a healing moment founded upon a vision beyond the material facts. Stephen Levine stated: "A healing moment is one in which the mind is not clinging to its passing show, not lost on the personal melodrama of its content, but tuned to the constant unfolding of the process in a moment of being fully *alive*," (1987, 32). This view is assisted by trusting the Generative Principle to provide the most appropriate unfolding.

Identifying with goodness at your being level is the most important conscious evaluation that you can make. The fact that you are good, whole and complete is an absolute, natural and permanent condition. Embracing the concept of *original sin* is damaging to self-esteem. The painful idea of original sin arrived along with the talking serpent in the Garden of Eden myth. Progressing through several millennia, the concept of *original goodness* provides a much more gratifying experience, especially when coupled with *original freedom* and *original love* to complement your spiritual identity. We do have knowledge of good and evil resulting from the evolution of conscious discrimination, but with it we can realize our inherent spiritual goodness.

Although this inherent goodness is the true characteristic of your conscious divinity, it cannot bring joy, satisfaction, and confirming manifestations unless you realize it. You must embrace the truth that you are intrinsically good in order for it to become a reality of your experience. The mental acceptance of your spiritual qualities appears simple, but it is not always easy. For example, you may associate with some prior worldly circumstances or behavior and conclude: *I know that I am not good because of all the terrible things that I have done.* Your Spiritual Self is independent of your human actions and previous worldly events, yet recollections of them can still distort your perspective.

You may think you need to go to a church, temple, or mosque in order to become spiritual, but you are *now* a spiritual being. Religious studies or worship may assist you in becoming aware of the being you already are, but your spiritual nature has already been bestowed upon you and no external authority can add to or detract from it. The final responsibility for this self-realization is yours, alone. The goodness of your basic nature is already established as your divine inheritance. Its magnitude is without bounds, with potential for manifesting in an inexhaustible number of ways.

Belief in goodness results in a better world through the emanation of the Generative Principle's creation of consequential experiences confirming these beliefs. Your realization of goodness grows, and is compounded as it is demonstrated in your daily affairs. Conversely, as you experience deprivation, beliefs in a lack of abundance can occur. Experience provides both *positive* and *negative* enforcement regarding ideas of benef-icence in that each evaluation released to your subconscious mind is acted upon by the formative powers of the Generative Principle. Such actions tend to produce validating experiences within the material world[2].

As shown in the diagram below, your evaluation of worldly per-ceptions gives rise to beliefs stored in the subconscious. Your sub-conscious mind lies within the Generative Principle. Beliefs become embodied within manifestations of the material world by way of Her creative principles that employ the appropriate natural laws of the universe. These new manifestations are then presented for your conscious perception and subsequent evaluation.

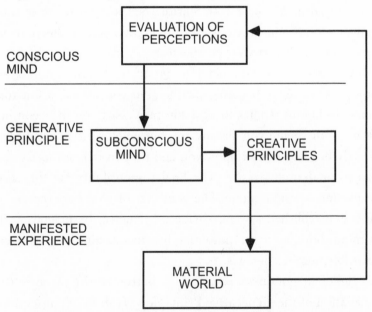

Figure 10. Conscious Enforcement through Manifestation of Beliefs

Whereas *patience* consciously acknowledges the potential of unseen goodness, faith is the subconscious counterpart. *Faith* is the belief in the goodness of life, sustaining us when we endure those long periods barren of goodness. As Kierkegaard terms it, faith is "the inner certainty that anticipates infinity," (1980, 157), the infinite potential of inner goodness.

Before a morning jog, a glass of fruit juice increases blood sugar, revs-up metabolism, and clears away cobwebs of sleep. In time, these carbohydrates burn away and the body calls upon the caloric reserves of stored fats and proteins accumulated at an earlier time. So it is with the experiences of life. Patience wears thin, as the saying goes, and during the trials of human experience, we must then rely upon our store of faith, which fuels the Generative Principle in providing us with the necessary sustenance and comfort.

Faith doesn't just happen. It is built up by attending to the nature of your Spiritual Self and accepting it as the truth of your being. You can develop faith by devoting time and energy to better know your Spiritual Self through meditating, counseling with a spiritual leader, and reading inspirational literature. But, most importantly, faith is developed by choosing personal action that is consistent with this belief. You empower convictions when you courageously put them into action, as courage is "faith in action."

You are a purveyor of goodness. Wholeness and well-being emerge as you call upon your inner resources and open yourself to the wellsprings of life. This understanding may occur as subtle intuitive knowing or it may appear as a new and grand idea. Spiritual fulfillment happens as your awareness is charged with a realization of life's values. Life is complete and sufficient unto itself. The realization of life's goodness leads to the joys of thanksgiving.

The Revelation of Love

As a Spiritual Being, you already are perfect, complete, and worthy. These qualities express through your own creativity. We are all linked in a holistic composition where each human expression is important and necessary. In your current existence, you are a singular, independent individual manifesting a unique human form. Yet, you are not alone in this earthly experience. We each make a distinctive representation in this communal stream of life. Differing beliefs resulting in divergent expressions provide us with a very interesting world, this being a testimony to the creativity of the universe.

The manifestation of each person has two-fold significance. First, every person's physical situation represents the Generative Principle's unique presentation appropriate for him or her. Second, another person's physical appearance *as seen by you* is a component of your manifested experience as delivered by the Generative Principle. In other words, you are responsible for *your* experience of every person, however they may appear. We share one world where experiences often have different subjective realities and meanings for each observer.

It is important to principally view your encounters with other people as being your experience rather than theirs because you can never see the world through their eyes. Even through empathy we can only partially understand another person's viewpoint. It is very easy to project the responsibility for your experience, e.g., *Look at what they are doing to me!* Yet, they are only serving as the Generative Principle's instruments replying to *your* subconscious content.

We are branches of the tree of life. We are rooted in spirit in the same qualities of goodness and freedom. The divergence of these branches attests to life's expansiveness. Life arises at birth into the air of consciousness, but cannot see backwards through the surface from which it sprang. The ground of our tree lies in obscurity. Through the millennia, it has been symbolically referred to as the Brahman, unnamable Tao, or the Great Mother. Emerson, in his essay *The Over-Soul*, simply stated: "Man is a stream whose source is hidden," (1926, 189).

Any goodness that we recognize in another is but an example of the inherent goodness within everyone. It is helpful, perhaps even necessary, to realize your own self-worth and to love yourself in order to respect and love another, for as the saying goes, "one cannot give from and empty vessel." Love is a synthesis of acknowledgment, understanding, acceptance, and appreciation for life. Through love, we revisit our interconnectedness. Love bridges the duality between yourself and others, thus allowing *oneness* to be realized. Empathy and compassion reflect in your human experience as a result of love.

Goodness is the *quality* of the basic life force acknowledged as a salute to the divinity within, as by a *Shalom* or *Namaste*, termed by Martin Buber as the Eternal Thou (1987, 75). Each of these terms represents an expression of love—a recognition and acceptance of the worthiness of another at the being level, unconditioned by worldly experience or by prior judgment. We do not have to like someone or their actions in order to look beyond appearance and recognize their inherent goodness. *Consciousness of the love connection is a natural, being-level identification with others.* The emotional responses accompanying this cognitive evaluation can also be termed love, although the word love has been employed to convey so many different emotions that its usage often appears trite and ambiguous (see Erich Fromm's *The Art of Loving*, 1956). Yet, no word, other than love, seems as appropriate to describe this *inter-psychic linkage* between beings. *Compassion*, as related to love, is a counterpart as applied to human situations.

Buber writes in *I and Thou*: "Feelings accompany the metaphysical and meta-psychical fact of love, but they do not constitute it," (1987, 14). And further: "Feelings dwell in man; but man dwells in love. This is no metaphor, but the actual truth. Love does not cling to the I in such a way as to have the *Thou* only for its 'content,' its object; but love is between *I* and *Thou*." Love refers to that connecting principle that unites individuals at the being level. The psychic invocation of love occurs as this unity is identified. In Buber's perspective, we do not distribute love to others. We only recognize it in our relationship with them.

Characteristics of your Spiritual Nature are pictured in a graphic relationship in the illustration shown below.

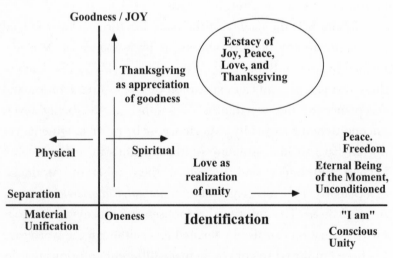

Figure 11. Characteristics of Your Spiritual Nature

Our internal realization of this *a priori* connection of love opens the channels of the universe so that the Generative Principle can distribute the revelations of goodness through grace to others. We may initiate the process in consciousness yet, despite our good intentions, we never do it alone. It can be a great relief to release the assumption that we can do it alone, and then to allow much greater powers and intelligence to assist us.

Your Expressive Nature

Your conscious activity initiates a response from the Generative Principle in creating experiences that provide you with a personalized expression and outward perspective. You, together with the Generative Principle and Her manifestations, form a composite triad participating in the vibrancy of life. She creates your experience, but has no control over your response following this experience. You, along with the Generative Principle, are co-creators of the universe. Whether your gender is male or female, in consciousness you express the function of the Father God archetype and, as such, you are subject to no *external authority*. You create your world of pleasure or pain, satisfaction or frustration, peace or fear, and heaven or hell. It's a tough job being a God, but everyone has to do it! Ralph Waldo Emerson summarized this important identity as that which "intellectually considered we call Reason, considered in relation to nature we call Spirit. Spirit is the Creator. Spirit hath life in itself. And, man in all ages and countries embodies it in his language as Father" (Dillaway, 1990, 57).

Relationships in this book have similarities to those of the German philosopher G. W. F. Hegel, who in 1807 wrote: "Identifications and separations of unchangeable essence [Spiritual Self in consciousness] and variable non-essence [physical manifestations] occur, which suggests the triune Persons of

Christian theology [as shown in the illustration below]. There is a consciousness, suggestive of the infinitely transcendent Father [Spiritual Self as it transcends physical world, also equivalent to Hegel's 'unchangeable essence']," (1977, 525). Regarding human awareness of physical manifestations, he wrote: "There is a consciousness, suggestive of the Son, which accepts something in the realm of unessential variability [phenomenal world] as an embodiment, an outer shape [personalized manifestation] of the unchangeable essence." Hegel recognized for the third aspect of the trinity, "a consciousness of the Spirit as reconciling the eternal essence with the changeable non-essence." Here, *Hegel's Spirit*, A. V. Miller's conventional translation of the German word *Geist*, is analogous to *the Generative Principle* used in this book.

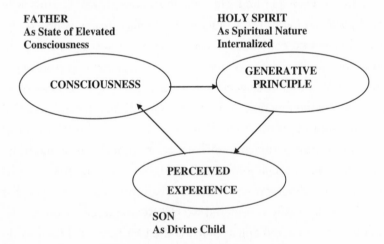

Figure 12. Analogy to Christian Trinity

Hegel respected the philosophical problem of dualism, where it is inconceivable how two distinct substances, the physical and non-material consciousness transcending the physical, can interact. Hegel (1977, 33) stated: "The substance of an existent thing is a self-identity or pure abstraction." He did not dismiss an *existent thing* as an abstract illusion, but rather termed it "a self-identity in otherness." Therefore, he would not likely object to calling material experience a *projection*, a concept further discussed regarding self-identity. Also, note that in his above interpretation of the Trinity, he referred to all three aspects as being forms of consciousness, suggesting Monistic Idealism[3]. During this period in religiously conservative Germany, Hegel prudently employed a fashionable theological language in his writings in order to maintain state and church approval for his academic positions.

The argument between Idealism and Materialism is a question of whether the reality of manifestations is mental or physical in character. This debate will likely continue with both sides claiming cause-and-effect relationships as evidence. Future science will likely provide us with new relationships to consider relative to this question. The introduction of the New Trinity, as a new spiritual ontology, mediates this apparent either/or duality by introduction of a third element: the Generative Principle as the common source for both phenomenal experience and consciousness of it. Rene Descartes recognized the need for an intermediary, but chose the God from his Jesuit schooling as the creative source, who set in motion an independent, mechanical universe not reflecting any interaction between consciousness, body, or experience.

David Chalmers in his book *The Conscious Mind* (1996, 161-171) suggests a *Natural Dualism*. This philosophical approach addresses the conundrum of explaining how non-material consciousness produces changes in the physical world. Science maintains that physical actions are logically required to produce material effects, a relation termed *causally closed*. Then, observed changes in the world produced by consciousness must occur through some, as yet unknown but *natural*, process rather than being physically *logical*—hence, the term Natural Dualism. In this book, this natural process is accomplished by the Generative Principle, which remains unknown except for the postulated functional characteristics.

Physical manifestations are here considered as a *valuable perspective to be taken seriously*; as material manifestations are necessary for creative expression. Although consciousness is considered as the *first cause* due to its volitional capability, it certainly is influenced by observations of the physical, so that the flow of effects continues in an involuted manner[4]. In any case, the appearance of the physical is a *real phenomenon* in conscious awareness.

French phenomenologist, Maurice Merleau-Ponty, described human relationships with the world as *intertwining*, objecting to any Cartesian separations between consciousness and worldly perceptions. For him, interactions between the corporeal body and environment were like an interwoven tapestry, stressing an experiential involvement with the living world (Moran, 2000, 403-409). Such a conceptual integration of mind and matter into a seamless web is necessary for any holistic view of life's processes.

In summary, *Spiritual Self* is an abstract term representing your innate quality and freedom. Yet, behind the static expression of language lies that dynamic, conscious being that you are. This Spiritual Self cannot be seen. Rather, it is a *state of being* having a subjective viewpoint from which you may see, know, and love both yourself and others. Aspects of your spiritual nature are shown in Table 1.

QUALITIES	CHARACTERISTIC	EFFECT
ETERNAL	Momentary existence in the here and now. Unconditioned by time and space.	Release from attachments. Freedom from anxiety. Equanimity.
FREEDOM	Singularity and exclusive freedom of will. Competency in conscious action.	Peace. Harmony. Composure.
GOODNESS	Inherent inner quality. Unconditioned receptiveness and openness to serendipity.	Joy. Thanksgiving. Manifestation of abundance.
LOVE	Realize unification within the divergence of life.	Appreciation and acceptance of others. Relationships.
THANKSGIVING	Realization of the presence of goodness.	Appreciation of life's experience.
EXPRESSIVE	Unending change in conscious expression.	Creativity and Unique expression.

Table 1. Qualities of your Spiritual Self

Dwelling upon your spiritual nature is important and merits priority in your schedule. As you establish self-identity as a spiritual being, you can demonstrate this view by exercising your capabilities as an active, caring human being. Levine observed that it is more difficult to learn how to have healthy interactions with other persons than to become a Saint, noting that Krishnamurti considered most Saints to be neurotic and not total human beings (1991, 69).

You are here on this earth for a very good reason with wonderful opportunities. Savor this experience! Maintain a perspective of your Spiritual Self while being aware of the human circumstance with "concernful" *interaction* with it, rather than *reaction*. Remember, you are alive and free as an unconditioned spiritual being. Be true to the goodness of your eternal nature.

Questions for Discussion

(1) As you encounter your spiritual identity, what type of experiences can you expect that will confirm this identity?

(2) Why is it important to address yourself in the first person, present tense as, "I am..."?

(3) What is your unique capability that distinguishes you from the Generative Principle in the creative process?

(4) How can you recognize and incorporate the freedom and goodness of your spiritual nature beyond an intellectual knowing? Why is this important?

(5) How do your beliefs manifest into experience?

(6) How does the concept of love as a uniting principle between spiritual beings compare with traditional views of love? Why is it not necessary to *like* people in order to *love* them?

Notes

[1] Sartre remained an atheist throughout his philosophical developments, and in his extensive exploration of consciousness never viewed it as embodying a spiritual nature. Likewise, he assigned little influence to the concept of subconscious mind or anything that might detract from the free will and ultimate responsibility of consciousness.

[2] Through freedom, you can also choose the opposite of good, which is often called *evil*. These two possible polarities resulting from volition were allegorically represented by Carl Jung as black and

white magicians, portraying the extremes of evaluation. He wrote: "The two magicians are, indeed, two aspects of the wise old man, the superior master and teacher, the archetype of the spirit, who symbolizes the pre-existent meaning hidden in the chaos of life. He is the father of the soul, and yet the soul, in some miraculous manner, is also his virgin mother, for which reason he was called by the alchemists the 'first son of the mother'" (1959, 35). *Father*, as the male god incarnate, willfully chooses good or evil. These recurring archetypes of consciousness tend to appear in myths and dreams as male figures relative to the feminine image, such as that of the Goddess. Such images do not represent some external authority, but the volitional aspect of divinity within your own consciousness.

[3]Another translator of Hegel, philosopher Walter Kaufmann, wrote: "Both Hegel and Nietzsche insisted on a metaphysical monism. They assumed that metaphysical inquiry has not been pushed to the limits as long as a thinker is confronted with two or more principles [as mental and physical]. Ultimately, any dualism has to be explained in terms of a single force" (1956, 206). Furthermore, "Hegel found the prototype of such a creative force in the Christian concept of the Holy Spirit which he interpreted in his own fashion," and which he considered as "essentially a process." Kaufmann explained: "Hegel's conception was derived from the Heilige Geist (Holy Spirit) which he considered as essentially a living and creative force" (1956, 385). We assign such characteristics to the single, active generative force.

[4]Conscious evaluation, as the *first cause*, is also the *efficient cause* in Aristotelian terms, followed by the *formative cause* as subconscious content within the formative Generative Principle, and the *material cause* as Her manifestations. Lastly, Aristotle's *final cause* is dependent upon subsequent conscious evaluation or personal significance, the latter fulfilling the purpose of manifestations.

CHAPTER 8

THE HUMAN CIRCUMSTANCE

Self-identification with the human form, contrasting with the unconditioned Spiritual Self, is a natural involvement with our worldly circumstance. This identity includes all physical events appearing to unfold in time and space, encompassing our bodies and defining our experiences. We reach back into the past to find meaning, anticipate the future for what it might bring, and wonder what is happening elsewhere that might affect us. We pack our memory with facts of science, economics, politics, and cultural expectations with the belief that such knowledge holds power that can assist in governing our destiny. Yet, we are confronted, again and again, with unexpected events that we cannot control. Attempts to encompass our human circumstance contribute little to the understanding of momentary existence in each *here and now*.

A World of Anxiety

The physical world is a creation of the Generative Principle. It is Her design, Her schedule, and Her message—following no rules except Her own. We may discern trends in the Generative Principle's design, but She tends to make unexpected moves that throw us off balance. Feeling uncomfortable with our lack of control, we question: *Now, how did that happen?* Alternatively, we may delight in Her surprises and appreciate Her novelty. We speak of good or bad experiences, though most physical events are a combination of both. The Generative Principle's simultaneous delivery of such experiences provides the tensions of human living, but also choices leading to growth.

As we concentrate on the present, our emotions become more simple and manageable. However, whenever we anticipate events *beyond* immediate sensory awareness, emotional response is always interlaced with *anxiety*. This is especially so whenever we attempt to think of how we can be affected by what *will* happen, what *has* happened, or what is happening at another place beyond our immediate vision. We want to *know about* and *control* the details of this imagined world beyond the present. Although we understand the impossibility of this task, we are not satisfied. And, though we generally do not particularly consider the Generative Principle being involved, *we want Her job.*

Anxiety is a fundamental *human* emotion resulting from the *uncertainty* of impending events. This uncertainty is the awareness that we do not, and cannot, completely understand or manage events of the world beyond immediate existence. Fluctuations of future and distant occurrences are largely indeterminate, and the control of external events, the past especially, is impossible. *Intelligence* and *power* are attributes of the Generative Principle. Human feelings of *unease* and *anxiety* occur due to our deficiencies in these faculties. The examination of anxiety is most important in understanding other emotions of the human experience.

We are acutely aware of anxiety when we attempt to anticipate significant happenings of the future, and then try to evaluate such events according to whether they will be good or bad for us. It has been facetiously advised that a way to avoid anxiety is to *have no expectations*—valid advice, but usually impractical. That which we anticipate *does not now exist* and *may never exist*. The goodness or badness of anything beyond the immediate present is merely an abstract potential existing only in the fantasy of mind. Because logic is always predicated upon and limited by the finite contents of awareness, uncertainty is inevitable in the human experience even when utilizing the best predictive logic.

Whereas our logic is limited to known associations of our restricted observations, the creative processes of the Generative Principle are *not*. The Generative Principle can always utilize a chain of events beyond our awareness that alters the obvious and expected outcome and, thus, we can only "expect the unexpected," as we never know what will develop. Anxiety is an emotion devoid of deterministic grounding, though one inherent to the human dilemma.

Anxiety is an emotion fundamental and exclusive to the Human Self, a component of all other emotions relevant to either the Favorable or Unfavorable World. Beyond simple expectation, *pure anxiety* has no particular focus. On the contrary, it involves ambivalence, and a general feeling of insecurity and unrest pending the Generative Principle's inevitable, but as yet undifferentiated, unfolding.

Anxiety moves away from this ambiguous position as we focus upon the occurrence of more concrete events with explicit judgments of good or bad. For example, *hope* involves an anticipation of something beneficial and desirable, whereas *fear* anticipates an adverse and unfavorable event. The emotions of hope and fear both vectorially include a degree of anxiety, but they differ in that they also include joy and anger, respectively, as shown in the following illustration.

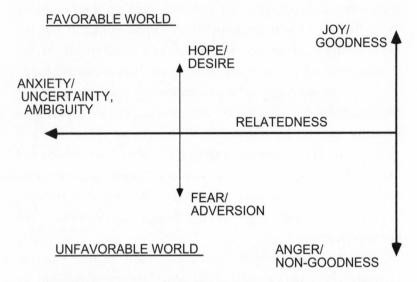

Figure 13. Polar Tensions of Emotions Relative to Uncertainties

Seventeenth century Dutch philosopher, Benedict Spinoza, was one of the first to systematically study the relationships of emotions. It is interesting to compare Spinoza's early model of emotions to the one proposed here. He wrote: "I, therefore, recognize only three primitive or primary emotions, namely, pleasure, pain, and desire" (Spinoza, 1955, 175). Examined utilizing the States of Conscious Evaluation, pleasure corresponds to the underlying judgment of goodness, and pain of non-goodness. Desire presumes a separation from the object of attention and, thus, includes a component of uncertainty and entails anxiety.

Fear can be considered to be the *polar opposite* of hope, and vice versa, as pictured in the above illustration. Spinoza insightfully commented: "[T]here is no hope unmingled with fear, and no fear unmingled without hope" (1955, 176). Realizing the subjectivity of emotion, he commented: "None of the objects of my fears contained in themselves anything either good or bad, except in so far as the mind is affected by them" (1955, 3). The world of experience entails both hopes and fears, and the individual is inevitably subjected to the *whims* and *vagaries* of natural forces. Such a dilemma is distinct from the paradoxical inner knowing that one's true self is free and independent of worldly constraints.

As illustrated below, there is a second, orthogonal type of polar tension contributing to anxiety in which the Conscious Self, efficacious in freedom of thought, views the constrained Human Self. The limitations of individual power in controlling externally manifested events contrasts with the autonomous command of personal thought, resulting in a tension within awareness as another root of anxiety. "Man, then," as described by Kierkegaard, "is a synthesis of the psyche [spirit] and body, but he is also a *synthesis of the temporal and the eternal*," (1980, 85), i.e., the *conditioned and the unconditionable*. Elsewhere Kierkegaard wrote: "How does the spirit relate itself to itself and to its conditionality? It relates itself as anxiety" (1980, 44).

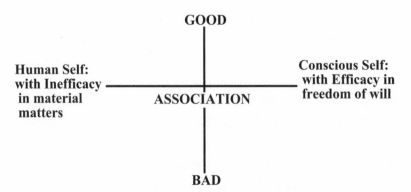

Figure 14. Polar Tensions of Efficacy Contrasting
the Conscious and Human Self

If you were solely defined by your human, physical body as a creature of time and space, then your physical situation would affect who you are, what you will be, and the quality of your future experience. To the extent that you believe that your identity is established only by your physical experience, you will continue to invest your emotional energies in the passing show. Yet, an inner part of you knows that your fate is not so deterministic. Realizing the permanency of spiritual goodness effects a mental healing of the outer experience. As noted by Stephen Levine, this facilitates "expanding the spaciousness of being, developing the deep patience that does not wait for things to be otherwise but relates with loving kindness to things as they are" (1987, 25). *Patience* is that position which abides in goodness even in the presence of conflicts.

Small children, for example, experience anxiety when they suspect that their mother is leaving them in the care of another. As she is the supplier of their physical and emotional needs, her absence generates a condition of uncertainty regarding their security. Similarly, we view *Mother Nature*, a personification of the Generative Principle, as the maternal source for all of our human needs. Deciding if She *is with us or not* becomes cause for anxiety.

When you forget your conscious identity and are absorbed by the limitations of human circumstances, you experience a lack of freedom. Even if choices are available, the exact outcome is never completely determined. This deficiency of material freedom results in imagining *what if* or *if only*, contrasting with freedom to move in thought. This is the conundrum of the generic man described by Reinhold Niebuhr: "In short, man, being both bound and free, both limited and limitless, is anxious. Anxiety is the inevitable concomitant of the paradox of freedom and finiteness in which man is involved" (1964, 182). Your worldly experience includes the components of your sensual perception and your imagination. Acknowledging your earthly experience while looking beyond it into your Conscious Self attends to the most important question of your life: your *total* self-identity.

In Western society, success is often qualified by personal, materialistic achievements. Criteria for accomplishment typically include the accumulation of possessions and wealth, personal appearance, cultural associations, physical capabilities, sexual conquests, social influence, academic credentials, and societal reputation. Establishment of self-worth, from the worldview, too often involves a comparison to others. In such a consensus reality, the competitive striving to arrive at the top requires *individual power* to overcome opposing worldly forces, with the outcome of this conflict remaining uncertain.

Fundamental questions, such as *Why am I here? What effect does my existence have in this world?* and *What is my worth?*, are dependent upon the thoughts about *who* you are, which, in turn, determine your emotional outlook. The formation of goals leading toward paths of worldly success constitutes a test of individual, egocentric capability, where the risk of failure becomes a threat to the ego. Self-esteem in this material environment depends upon personal action, coupled with chance opportunities. Here, self-worth is affected by standards imposed by an external society, rather than by internal or absolute factors. Through this material perspective, we see environment as being restrictive to individual growth.

The early writings of Freud, as reviewed by Rollo May (1977, 132-148), maintained that anxiety originated from the *trauma of birth* or from a *fear of castration*. Although few people now support these theories in the literal sense, Freud perhaps had an intuitive insight as he advocated the earthy symbols of birth and castration as a basis for anxiety. Birth trauma can be metaphorically interpreted as a *separation from source of supply*, and castration fear as a *loss of potency or power*. As human beings, we are dependent upon external sources and have limited power to meet all of our physical needs. As a result, we are anxious about the human dilemma.

Not all anxiety originates from such conscious reflection, however. Some results from emanations of the subconscious. Possible threats, imagined with an unbearable degree of fear or pain, may become repressed so that they are no longer within awareness. But, repressed ideas, accompanied by strong emotion, tend to eventually manifest themselves. Eventually, the Generative Principle will reveal repressed emotion. Some new thing or event becomes a character on our stage, clothed appropriately for projection, and playing a role invoking anxiety. If others consider our emotional response to be inappropriate, then our action may be labeled as *neurotic*. Yet, no one else can experience our projection as we do. To us, our response is very appropriate.

Anxiety labeled as neurotic usually involves the repression of situations seen as threats to security or personal good, implying a risk to self-worth or capability to function. Seldom is a *good* experience repressed, although it can be if we feel that we don't deserve something or have been taught that it is *wrong*. For example, one who has been raised in an overly Puritanical environment may find it difficult to express joy. In this example, the Shadow might appear through us as a Bacchanal trickster acting from a repressed desire for revelry.

Repression frequently results from difficult experiences of childhood, which are unconsciously carried forward into adult years. Psychologists who have studied anxiety, such as Rollo May (1977), believe that persons have a greater disposition toward neurosis if they have experienced rejection from their parents, especially their mothers. Since children have fewer interpersonal skills and are ill-equipped to cope with intolerable situations, they are more likely to repress threats and, thus, obtain order in their lives through mental dissociation. In adulthood, the original situation resulting in repression usually may long since have been forgotten and is now inaccessible.

Potential manifestations of repressed beliefs sometimes lie just below the threshold of awareness and bring feelings such as an impending threat or doom. At such times, one experiences a general emotion of anxiety prior to the actual occurrence of a projected event since they arise from the same source. This anxiety may be a precursor to the intuitively anticipated manifestation, so that awareness has no actual object upon which to reflect. An outside observer might judge such an anxious response as unfitting, yet the potency of anyone's experience lies not only with the event itself, but also from emotions originating from unseen, historical associations, values, and beliefs.

The emotion of anxiety can swing from hope to fear. This oscillation is a source of physical and mental agitation that can be either exciting or disturbing. For example, I was driving one day to my office following an extended trip, expecting to encounter some usual surprises along with newly arising problems. The polar extremes of my anxiety included *exhilaration* and *unease*, while knowing that whatever problems existed would present a challenge to which the organization could ably respond. Indeed, there were some favorable reports, as well as a challenging problem involving an important employee who resigned to change careers. Following initial misgivings and apprehension regarding the resignation of this significant employee, the question, *How do we cope?* served as a catalyst in mobilizing creative energies that resulted in a more effective organization. So often, little crises are very useful in moving us beyond a comfortable status quo and on to a new perspective. Evaluation of an anxiety-producing situation depends upon how we believe our self to be affected; that is, whether we view the event to be enhancing or harmful. When identity shifts to the Spiritual Self, outward events are viewed by an involved, but unattached, stationary observer.

Encountering Goodness

When things appear to be going really great, I feel like singing, *It's a wide, wide, wonderful world*, don't you? When things are going well for us, our hearts are so much lighter. We receive our life gently, similar to the melody of a song. Greet and appreciate your experiences whenever possible without attachment, possession, or personal identification and feel your heart sing!

To assume that the *personal self* is solely responsible for worldly achievements discounts the powers of the Generative Principle. The attachment of the ego identity to worldly accomplishments must be relaxed in recognizing a spiritual identity, and in realizing that spiritual efficacy occurs as a union with the Generative Principle. Recognition of both physical and conscious capabilities forms a valid basis for the psychological adage that *one must establish an ego before releasing it.* You do play a most important part in the process, but you do not do it alone.

In the Favorable World State, goodness manifests itself in your experience through the many forms of impermanent physical pleasures and worldly happiness. In addition to these corporeal manifestations, you can experientially encounter goodness in numerous conscious activities. In all cases you pursue, encounter, and depart from the actual or envisioned successes of your life that appear as earthly fulfillment. It is ironic, yet informative, that as these successes are achieved attention usually shifts elsewhere.

It is easy to find people with wealth, fame, physical beauty, and intelligence who become dissatisfied with their lives, no matter what their accomplishments. This provides a clue that a lasting sense of joy and fulfillment comes from within, rather than without. Worldly happiness is an ephemeral type of joy, like a child receiving a piece of candy, a source of brief gratification. Experiences offer transitory delights that, if held too long, become stale like week-old pastry.

Enjoy smelling the flowers and all worldly fruitions, realizing that such things represent manifestations of goodness, rather than its source. And, in actuality, to *really* smell the flowers is not a trivial matter. It requires a dedication of attention, not only to the senses but also to the emotional *feeling* of the experience. It is certainly worthwhile to pursue secular achievements through diligent activities of your mind and body, as this is the natural process for *demonstrating* and *appreciating* inner goodness. Discovering worldly enjoyments is a game we, humans, are here to play.

Believing that physical things, events, or relationships are necessary for the enhancement of our human lives, we mentally assign them worth and meaning, thereby forming *attachments* and relying on these temporal objects to supply us with worldly goodness. Such profit from external sources does not enhance our Conscious Self, which is always complete within itself. Instead, it is merely a complement for the outer human shell. Material attachments in their sundry forms, and our dependence upon them, characterize both the Favorable and Unfavorable Worlds.

In seeking material goodness for the benefit of another person, perhaps supplying them with what we think they need, our satisfaction can become conditional upon their well-being—if serving *their* need becomes *our* need through such attachments. In this way, a seemingly altruistic effort can form a condition commonly known as *codependency*, termed by Dr. Timmen Cermak "a disease of relationships" (1986, 104). "Power through sacrifice of Self lies at the core of codependency" (1986, xii), wrote Cermak, although it is possible to engage in benevolent actions through the *giving of love without attachment*, as will be addressed later.

In the Favorable World State, we are often separated from an attractive object of desire, with relationship determined either by distance, future time, past time, or potential occurrence. For example, we may lack the right job, money, good health, or a wished-for relationship. Such things that we believe would fill a deficiency and bring joy and happiness. Alternatively, we may have had something in a past experience that provided us with a vital complement, such as the prowess and beauty of youth, something whose time has passed and we no longer possess in original form.

Experiences within the Favorable World, as shown on the following illustration, occur in a three-stage cycle, as we (1) approach that which we identify as good, (2) have contact with it, and (3) depart from it; with degrees of uncertainty existing through all three stages. As we advance toward a desired object, we anxiously wonder: *Will I obtain it?* Upon acquisition, we ask: *Can I maintain it?* And, following dispossession, we question: *What will replace it?*

The degree of uncertainty depends upon the statistical likelihood of an event's occurrence and upon our subjective expectations. By expecting, we are looking beyond the here and now, beyond the present moment, and ignoring the immediate message of the Generative Principle by directing our attention out there. Anxiety can be reduced or eliminated by coming into full contact with the current experience through sensing and feeling, rather than thinking about and speculating.

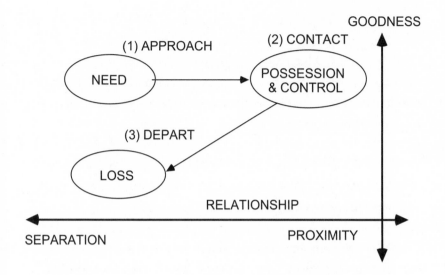

Figure 15. Three Cycles of Attachment in the Favorable World State

In Pursuit of Goodness—First Stage of Attachment

Immersed in sensory experiences of earth, we become aware of physical deficiency and material incompleteness. Words and ideas we use to represent this human predicament include lack, restriction, incompletion, and inadequacy. These are all concepts based on goodness beyond immediate grasp. Human concerns frequently involve acquiring something, such as financial security or a suitable personal relationship. The successes of other parties, individuals, or institutions sometimes accentuate our lack of perceived goodness, as in, *He has the talent* (or money and relationships), *but I don't*, or *My finances are in a mess because of the economy*. There always seems to be a rational explanation as to why we are not perfectly fulfilled, with the world seeming less than ideal. As we need, want, or hunger for distant goodness in this first stage of attachment, associated passions range through hope, desire, impatience, craving, lust, or greed.

The idea of restriction, embodied as belief, then manifests itself as a blockage or impediment to acquisition of the desired. Manifestations, which always represent kernels of belief, confirm and enforce the original value judgment. A master spiritual psychologist, as reported in the book of Matthew, expressed this *principle of reinforcement*:

> *For whosoever hath, to him shall be given, and he shall*
> *have more abundance: but whosoever hath not, from him*
> *shall be taken away even that which he hath.*

This principle may appear unfair until it is recognized to be under the control of consciousness. Many situations are like a carrot dangling on a stick just beyond reach: *If I could get a better job, I could catch up on my bills*; or *If the right person walked into my life, I wouldn't be so lonely*. In order to remove the belief in conditions, one must remove the separation in time and space between the self and goodness. A simple suggestion would be to enjoy the job that you have, and you will find a job that you like. But, this idea may promote the fear, *I might get stuck in the job that I have*, still meaning that *something better for me is out there*. Developing security through identification with the internal and immediate goodness of the Spiritual Self involves no external conditions and provides a more enduring solution. Goodness then manifests accordingly in physical experience.

A person acquiring some knowledge regarding the principles of belief and its effect upon experience might correctly say, *I hold subconscious beliefs that make it difficult for me to develop a good relationship,* and continue *but I am working to find the root cause and eliminate it in order to free myself*. However, he is still perpetuating the power of a limiting condition and holding it beyond his immediate access. He could possibly work for years pursuing the *root cause*. Such a struggle would more likely strengthen the subconscious opposition, perhaps even intensifying its undesirable effects, until the immediacy of *available* goodness within the Conscious Self is recognized. Such recognition would, thereby, initiate a new belief. Beliefs in limiting conditions are dissolved only as new beliefs in fulfillment are generated, contradicting and displacing the old.

A belief in limitation might have a *specific* root, such as early parental introjections: *You can never get ahead in this society*, or *Fairytale romances just don't happen in real life.* Yet, the origin of subconscious content really doesn't matter anymore. The *elemental* ideas underlying limiting beliefs are often relatively simple: *There is limited goodness in this world, so expect to suffer.* Or, *I do not deserve more goodness in this world.* It is usually a wasted effort to seek the original cause because some cognizant equivalent may be inferred from current experiences and addressed in the present.

It is easy to understand why many people arrive at a belief in limited goodness. But, goodness is a quality rather than a thing and is not restricted to a particular medium for human realization. Whereas our human perspective is extremely narrow due to our finite awareness, the Generative Principle, as the ultimate provider, is unlimited in Her creativity and resources.

If you say, *I do not deserve*, who is this I to which you are referring and who ordained this judgment? Certainly it is not the I of your Spiritual Self, which is inherently good and eternally maintaining its nature. It can only be the *I* of your egoistic self, your own worldly creation. As ego does not have a mind separate from your own, you are its sole judge and spokesperson. Just shift your perspective from the external to the internal, become aware of and accept the qualities inherent in your spiritual nature, and rely upon the power and intelligence of the Generative Principle. Here, you will find the open door to the experience of goodness.

Managing Material Success—Second Stage of Attachment

Beliefs in deserved goodness tend to manifest into experiences that, in turn, bring a sense of fulfillment and happiness. This second stage of material attachment is where you attain possessions, accomplish goals, achieve success, or consummate a relationship. Excitement, happiness, satisfaction, appreciation, and a feeling of belonging are positive emotions typically resulting from pleasurable contact with demonstrated goodness.

To paraphrase Meister Eckhart, *if the only prayer you say in your life is 'thank you,' that will suffice*. It is essential to acknowledge and appreciate material blessings as the Generative Principle's confirmation that *life* is good. Thanksgiving is the joy of receiving, requiring acceptance, realizing the value of goodness. Communication is a bilateral action: The Generative Principle speaks through Her manifestations, yet if experiences are not fully received with appropriate regard, the communication is incomplete. Each experience is to be valued with gratitude at the moment it is received. Too often, we are preoccupied with anticipation of the *next* development or with what happened *last*, rather than acknowledging what is immediately before us.

Unfortunately, desirable material objects and relationships are often seen as things to be possessed and controlled, mistaking such things as a source, rather than a demonstration of goodness. Life is simpler and more pleasant when we lightly acknowledge human pleasures, and then release them. Life as a spiritual being consists of moment-to-moment renewals, where attachments are unnecessary baggage. When self-identity is associated with the human experience, and self-worth is linked to the adopted material values of society, then self-esteem is lowered if we have less than we think we need. For example, having financial difficulties, losing approval of a significant person, becoming physically incapacitated, or just making a serious mistake, can become a devastating experience if one's self-validation is dependent upon external factors.

Conversely, if we have *more* in comparison to others, we may egotistically interpret our position as being superior and feel arrogant or grandiose, confusing possessions and achievements with self-worth. In this scenario, one's self-evaluation vacillates whenever material fortunes change. Pia Mellody offers an alternative perspective: "Healthy self-esteem is the internal experience of one's own preciousness and value as a person," (1989, 7).

We can enjoy life much more fully if we encounter it as a continuous flow. Despite all our attempts to grasp ephemeral attachments, human reality is more like the journey of Ulysses as described by Alfred Lord Tennyson:

> *Yet all experience is an arch where through*
> *Gleams that untraveled world whose margin fades*
> *Forever and forever when I move.*
> *How dull it is to pause, to make an end,*
> *To rust unburnished, not to shine in use!*

Since the quality of physical experience is so important to our egoistic identity, it is understandable that people attempt to *control* worldly circumstances. It has been a popular belief since the Renaissance that through intellect and personal capabilities humans can master natural forces and triumphantly achieve dominion over material situations. A personification of the hero in our society—whether warrior, politician, business executive, or popular entertainer—is one who strides forth conquering obstacles, a person whose efficacy is measured by *worldly* gains. Yet, the hero need not *make an end* in such gains, but with thankful acknowledgment, continue ahead and *shine in use*.

At the same time, development of personal capabilities is a practical human endeavor not to be depreciated. Difficulties arise *only* when a person views himself or herself as a singular entity in achieving satisfaction, further inflating the Ego. When acquiring of material gratification is perceived as conquest, domination, or superior position, then emotions of triumph, pride, conceit, vanity, and self-righteousness arise. The Generative Principle often accomplishes Her undertaking through our personal actions, with the part we play being very important, yet accomplishments are made only through Her design.

When material welfare is achieved, the sense of personal accomplishment and security is only transitory because of the fluidic nature and impermanence of all things physical, and where unexpected changes by Mother Nature can produce a great deal of frustration. Real and permanent security, sufficient to sustain peace of mind, is derived only from the internal identification with, and acceptance of, goodness of the conscious being, the Spiritual Self. Randomness and uncertainty are fundamental to the nature of the physical world, therefore providing flexibility for manifestations of the Generative Principle.

Frustrations in human pursuits reveal limited freedom and capability. However, an important distinction is to be made between *material* freedom and *conscious* freedom. Material freedom is restricted to that pathway prepared by the Generative Principle, whereas consciousness can move freely among all options known to awareness. The need to recognize this volitional freedom, distinguishing it from restricted earthly pathways, is the basis for the Serenity Prayer:

> *God grant me the serenity to accept the things I cannot change; courage to change the things I can; and wisdom to know the difference.*

A most precious attribute of consciousness is the ability to make willful decisions, although the term *will power* can be misleading. We are empowered with mental capabilities used to form beliefs that are acted upon by the powers of the Generative Principle. Worldly power relies upon the Generative Principle, so that *human efficacy* is actually a cooperative effort. The humbling realization of this fact changes the statement of *I can*, to *We, the Generative Principle and I, can, or I (Human Self) can, Generative Principle is willing.*

Human self-confidence is the conviction that through personal *means* and abilities, goals *can* be achieved and needs be met. As long as the means are understood to be a cooperation of natural forces beyond the individual, this conviction is valid. It is readily observable that people who believe that they can accomplish something are more likely to do so. This belief tends to manifest the necessary forces and processes, *especially* when the believer employs both mental and physical action toward a goal.

Mercurial Goodness—Third Stage of Attachment

There is an infinite variety of goodness available for manifestation, but with no single form enduring. As expressed in Ecclesiastes (3: 1), "To everything there is a season, and a purpose under heaven." Our mercurial goodness occurs in a particular form during its season, and then changes. Still, goodness is a *quality* and never a particular thing. Or, from another view, manifested goodness is "a many-splendored thing," whose form is continually changing like light passing through a revolving kaleidoscope.

From our human vantage point, *goodness changing* sometimes appears as *goodness lost*, especially when we have become attached to a particular form. As manifested forms of goodness inevitably change, a concept of loss occurs that characterizes the third stage of attachment. That which was once seen as the source of satisfaction or pleasure becomes distant in time or space. Likewise, the displaced joy, now existing only in memory, is felt in degrees of sadness. Fulfilling the cycle from *dust to dust*, empires, bouquets of flowers, and relationships disintegrate when their time has passed. In this reflective stage, emotions may range from melancholy, to sorrow, to extreme grief, with the Favorable World slipping into the Unfavorable World view.

Events such as opportunities lost due to a lack of self-confidence, health lost to disease, business ventures lost because of changing economic conditions, a lover lost to disillusionment, or a family member lost to an automobile accident are lamentable, but typical of human experience for which we inevitably feel degrees of mournfulness. When these separations occur, there is no immediate escape from the painful emotional consequences because such emotions are linked to the event. Some solace is found in the realization of your spiritual identity, but even so, another part of you is still human and feels loss. This is the time to acknowledge the wound and feel the grief until its time has passed. Consolation occurs in realizing your Spiritual Self as eternal, beyond material impermanence, and composed of goodness with a quality that never fades. All perceptions of loss occur only in the physical world of experience, whereas intrinsic reality lies in the realm of consciousness. The goodness of your Spiritual Self may dim in your awareness, but is indestructible and can sustain no loss.

A more manageable form of loss is self-inflicted under the guise of self-sacrifice. Certainly, some forms of sacrifice are necessary for survival when, for example, there is little food in the house and the children are starving. Sacrifice, as religious offering, may be beneficial to the psyche. However, self-sacrifice is sometimes practiced in support of a false belief that there is not enough good to go around, typically, e.g., *I had better give up mine so that you will be okay.* This does not recognize the freedom and capability of each individual to manifest *his or her own abundant expression* in this universe. There is an unlimited amount of goodness within every person available through realization, and which only he or she can call forth into experience. Their habitual reliance upon the self-sacrifice of others may perpetuate the idea of limitation, inhibiting their realization of goodness. A most appropriate gift for one in need is an encouragement toward self-reliance. Yet, your charitable gift from a realization of love and abundance can be an uplifting experience for both parties.

Questions for Discussion

(1) Why is *anxiety* a fundamental emotion of the human circumstance, and what is the underlying condition that causes it?

(2) What fundamental value judgment is common to all emotions of the Favorable World State?

(3) Why do the polar opposites of *hope* and *fear* both involve a component of anxiety?

(4) As a favorable object is approached, in the first cycle of attachment of the Favorable World State, what emotions are typically encountered?

(5) As the object is *encountered* in the second cycle of attachment, what are typical associated emotions?

(6) What emotions are likely to occur as the object *departs* in the third cycle?

CHAPTER 9

BITTER FRUITS OF WORLDLY KNOWLEDGE

One of my favorite fables involves a King who summoned his wise men, commanding them to write an inscription for his ring, which upon his reading would cause him to smile when things were bad and to be sad when things were good. After some meditation and consultation, they returned to the King with the inscription, "This too shall pass." Through the eternal cycle of change, we tend to cling to the most pleasant of circumstances, rather than to simply appreciate the good times while they occur and then release them when their time has passed.

The Up Side of Down

Commenting upon the Biblical imperative to Adam: "Only from the tree of the knowledge of good and evil you must *not* eat," Kierkegaard wrote, "The prohibition induces in him [Adam] anxiety [translation of *angst*], for the prohibition awakens in him freedom's possibility...the anxious possibility of *being able*" (1980, 44). You are *free and able* to experience the bitter as well as the sweet fruits of the world, evoking associated degrees of anxiety. As a human capable of evaluating each experience, the knowledge of good and evil is unavoidable. That said, to judge the essence of your own being as bad or evil is absolutely incorrect, and the idea of *original sin* as often interpreted from this story of Adam is a false concept dangerous to your mental health. The admission of original sin is accompanied by the unjust existential emotion of *guilt* as an unnecessary self-condemnation.

The term *angst*, used by Kierkegaard and some other existential philosophers and here translated as *anxiety*, is sometimes translated as *anguish*. Anguish refers to a painful emotion concerning conscious freedom in making decisions and agonizing over whether choices meet the approval of a transcendental God. The self-doubt and insecurity in the presence of such a judgmental deity can result in the mental pain of anguish. How different is the meeting of unobstructed conscious freedom found in the security of the Spiritual Self. Here, the resulting emotion is peace in absence of worldly expectations and conflict. The term *anxiety* will be reserved for emotions related to a general encounter of uncertainty in the physical world. The unavoidable emotion of anxiety need not result in anguish.

In our model of conscious evaluation, as was pictured in Figure 5, both the state of Elevated Consciousness and the state of Favorable World have in common the judgment of goodness, with the remaining states sharing the evaluation of non-good, unfavorable, bad, or evil. Associated with every undesirable or bad experience is a degree of *anger* in some form or variation. Whether acknowledged or suppressed, this anger is an inevitable emotional response toward that which is perceived as not good. A moderate discomfort, irritation, or dissatisfaction, for example, can result in a mild form of anger or annoyance. More often, however, anger is a vector component contained within another emotion and is not identified in its pure form. For instance, fear is a response to possible threat, where the actual event has not yet occurred and remains distant and uncertain. The emotion of fear, then, involves anxiety toward a potential threat and latent anger.

Many believe that anger is a useless, negative emotion to be avoided. By denying and suppressing anger, one may appear outwardly calm yet remain inwardly disturbed. Anger is the natural emotional response toward something judged as bad, but there is nothing inherently bad about feeling angry. It is often our behavior in response to an emotion such as anger that causes a problem.

Anger-management programs, for example, more frequently address enraged, explosive, and inappropriate *actions* resulting from our response to anger. Such behavior, often uncontrolled and irrational, causes suffering to ourselves and others, and needs to be distinguished from underlying emotions and placed under control. Here, it is more productive to understand the underlying cause of annoyance or frustration and, with patience and self-compassion, find more constructive behavior as an alternative to *losing one's temper*.

Denying emotion is, at best, only a temporary reprieve. An experience that is repressed must later be re-presented to consciousness so that the Generative Principle's message may be heard. *As humans*, we never outgrow the emotion of anger, although we may develop understanding and tolerance that moderates the judgment of a situation as being bad, thereby diminishing anger. Significantly, in the spiritual state of Elevated Consciousness, where one's essential nature is affirmed, anger does not and cannot exist.

Every experience is a case of *self-meeting-self*, in the sense that the Generative Principle animates experience from one's own beliefs. Commonly, we project onto other people the cause of dissension, rather than assume personal responsibility. But, these people are only components of physical manifestation. The real cause of discomfort lies within an inaccessible and unknown personal belief. To function efficiently in social and business relationships, we can acknowledge our anger and then proceed to either accept or change the immediate offensive situation. We can then begin to address the underlying beliefs.

Encountering Worldly Discord

In the State of Unfavorable World, we frequently encounter material circumstances contrary to our preference. The difference between the Favorable and Unfavorable World is not determined by objective, quantitative measurement. Instead, it is due to subjective response through qualitative judgment. We view bad events as if they were opposed to goodness, rather than simply an evaluation of *goodness deficiency*. As we transform these value judgments and emotional feelings into physical behavior, we are *attracted* to the rewards of the Favorable World; whereas we usually avoid the threats of the Unfavorable.

Approaching Threats

Three stages of *negative* attachment toward non-goodness in the Unfavorable World parallel the *positive* attachments to goodness of the Favorable World. As goodness diminishes, the situation can appear as threatening. For instance, if a loved one becomes ill and death seems imminent, fear of loneliness likely will occur. In this first stage of negative attachment, objects are interpreted as being a risk, hazard, possible danger, or potentially adverse. Yet, these threats remain only as possibilities since the outcome is uncertain.

Receding goodness is the *third stage* of positive attachment of the Favorable World. However, when the same situation is perceived as increasing non-goodness, it becomes the *first stage* of *negative* attachment within the Unfavorable World, as illustrated here.

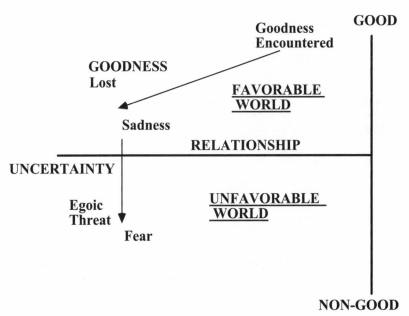

Figure 16. Transformation of Loss into Fear

Egoistic attachment moves to the front of awareness when a symbol of personal value and status has been lost. The world then appears less favorable and, perhaps, a threat to personal values that is typically accompanied by fear and anger.

As goodness recedes, the mind anticipates a negative consequence, even though a threat may not actually be apparent. Potential danger may be either unreasonably magnified or underestimated in the imagination. Therefore one's initial response is possibly inappropriate to the eventual encounter. We invoke the negative side of anxiety, namely *dread*, in viewing an impending situation having some threatening potential. Fritz Perls (1976, 20) expressed it as follows: "The dreadful is experienced as vague, undifferentiated danger; as soon as there is an object to cope with [real or imagined], dread diminishes into fear."

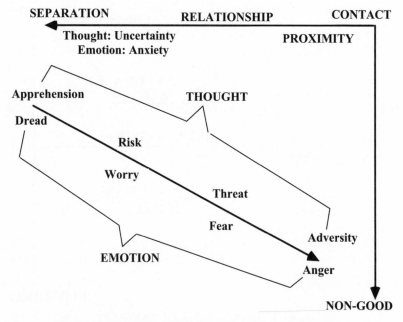

Figure 17. Variation of Emotion in Approach to Adversity

Prior to contact, an emotion of anxiety underlies the possibility of either good or bad. Human aliveness feeds upon this tension as anxiety embodies both hope and dread. As uncertainty is reduced, "dread diminishes into fear." Then, as the threat is actually encountered, fear, itself, dissolves into one of the many forms of anger as pictured below.

As long as self-identity is associated with physical experience, we are susceptible to the continual changes. Kernels of belief incorporating ideas of diminished goodness eventually manifest in uncomfortable experiences, threatening our sense of fulfillment. Ideas of self-competency, in contrast to vulnerability, produce an entirely different set of beliefs and manifestations that, with diligent action and good intentions, usually lead to satisfactory results. Through beliefs embodying self-confidence, the Generative Principle tends to empower us over adversity.

Confronting the Threat

The term *contact boundary*, borrowed from Gestalt Therapy, figuratively represents a confrontation where the situation, judged either good or bad, is met in the *here* and *now*. Fritz Perls wrote: "Contacting the environment is, in a sense, forming a gestalt" (1976, 23), that is, forming a unified whole. The contact or near contact with an undesirable object characterizes the second stage of negative attachment, with the separation by time or distance diminishing, or probability of occurrence increasing, as we arrive at the contact boundary.

As the proximity to the adversary increases, either physically or in imagination, the potential for anger intensifies. The apparent continuum of time is reduced to the instant of *now*, with no other space except the immediate. To truly be in the present moment, and in existential contact with the event, is to be without anticipation of future possibilities and associated fears. Anger becomes the dominant emotion in face-to-face contact with an ominous manifestation. Anger is the polar opposite of joy and is, to varying degrees, a component of all other emotions in the Unfavorable World. Anger can range from mild annoyance to enragement.

Visualize the young boy who is frequently intimidated by a larger bully, antagonized to the point where he charges forth enraged, swinging his fists in anger, disregarding the consequences. The bully stumbles backwards in shock, then turns and retreats from this wild, uninhibited assailant. As the boy's anger subsides, he slumps to the ground wondering and worrying about what will happen tomorrow when he encounters the bully again. Fear can arise again only as we anticipate what might happen in the future. It is maintained here that anger is the natural and fundamental emotion corresponding to a judgment of non-goodness, the opposite of joy. Anger can be actualized into a mobilizing force involving either constructive or destructive action for changing the circumstances or eliminating the threat. Confronting a threat is often recommended as a way for overcoming fear as it can serve to deliver us from adversity. Anger is, thereby, more useful than other emotions of the Unfavorable World. We may respond to a threat with flight rather than fight. Flight or retreat transports us away from the encounter, usually in fear, whereas fight occurs as we confront the threat in anger. Or, we may remain frozen in fear and anxiety. Regarding the fight or flight option, some behaviorists, such as Plutchik (1991, 75-84), believe fear and anger to be opposite emotions because the actions of flight and fight, or retreat and aggression, propel a person in opposite spatial directions. Yet, *spatial* directions do not correspond to psychic dimensions. The contrasting position of this book is that emotions have a direct correspondence to conscious evaluation, and that fear and anger are closely related through the common evaluation of something being bad, and *can occur together*. But fear involves a component of anxiety, while *pure* anger does not. Fear can be visualized geometrically as a vector composed in varying degrees of both anxiety and anger. Aggressive behavior need not be destructive as it can be instrumental in constructive problem solving. For example, a courageous fireman aware of danger and in the face of fear, yet also with compassion and a desire to help, might aggressively chop down a door to rescue trapped individuals.

We cannot continually avoid thoughts of the past and future, yet it is important to remember that achievements and meaningful experiences occur only in the immediate space of the present moment. We accomplish things with no anxiety if we maintain focus upon the here and now. Perls wrote: "If you are in the now, you can't be anxious because the excitement flows immediately into ongoing spontaneous activity. If you are in the now, you are creative, you are inventive. If you have your senses ready, if you have your eyes and ears open, like every small child, you will find a solution" (1971, 3).

> True satisfaction is found by acting in the moment,
>
> appreciating that which is fulfilling, and working
>
> to change that which is found dissatisfying.

Contacting the immediate experience, you differentiate *what is relative to what could be or what might have been.* You live fully by attending to that which is set before you, whereas you have no efficacy over the past or future.

We identify adversity as that which causes us pain or discomfort. Personal growth through change occurs by encountering adversity, opposition, discord, or resistance where discontent sometimes facilitates a transformation. Unfortunately, there are unpleasant circumstances that we cannot overcome by physical means. The fact of human life is that we do not always win in a worldly sense. Human defeats and even death are pathways of the Generative Principle where we all eventually end our tenure on earth. An encounter with adversity need not always be one of aggressive conquest. Even though our initial response may entail fear and anger, there is an alternative to the fight-or-flight reaction: *The path of surrender to the Way of the Generative Principle.* Eventually, She alone will prevail as our consciousness is released from this earthly sojourn. We can, to the anguish of Dylan, "go gentle into that good night."Yet, there are many other occasions prior to this final moment where surrender is a viable option.

Surrender is not a popular choice in Western culture where we seek to prevail over nature, even though at times it is the most graceful response. To yield to a humanly painful outcome, under some circumstances, is the highest form of non-attachment, acknowledging material impermanence while affirming an underlying spiritual reality. One occasion when surrender may seem appropriate is when you are incapacitated with pain, either physically or mentally. Occurrences of pain are experientially real and can dominate awareness and saturate your senses. On such occasions it is expeditious to meet intense pain directly with acceptance rather than resistance, acknowledging its presence, and blessing and forgiving its circumstances. With humility, you can invite it to reveal its message and soon depart, knowing that all such things are temporal and will pass when their time is complete. We sometimes realize that painful circumstances cannot be altered through the efficacy of our consciousness. This can be an occasion to release to Soul, to the Way of Tao, to providence, or to "die unto the world."

During these distressing times, a philosophic approach may have to wait until you are able to separate the painful encounter from the observing self. Pain, seen objectively, is rationally and legitimately a threat. Yet, *to what is it a threat?* That which is threatened is the physically manifested Human Self, rather than the eternal Spiritual Self. Threats may endanger the body, but have no other power over consciousness except to disrupt awareness. Spiritual Self is neither defined by, nor opposed by, the physical world and, therefore, cannot be threatened by it. True security is found only in associating identity with the spiritual, conscious being.

Disengaging from the Threat

In the third stage of negative attachment of the Unfavorable World, we disengage from adversity either with mindful action or through repression. We can engage the threat and overcome it, alter the circumstances, or dwell within the discordant event as it completes its natural cycle. As an example of the last case, I contract a head cold, am inconvenienced for a week, and finally heal through my body's immunity process. When its time has passed, the issue departs from awareness.

Retreating from the contact boundary through physical or mental flight prematurely terminates a disagreeable situation, potentially resulting in an incompletion. In an uncomfortable encounter with a family member, I might just change the subject, *sweep it under the carpet*, or forget it. Such an incompletion does not eliminate the problem, but rather leaves it unresolved within subconsciousness. Events found extremely damaging to self-image are likely to be repressed and no longer accessible to recall. However, the Generative Principle only temporarily allows such incompletion. She repeats her messages until they are heard.

An emotionally impactful encounter, such as abandonment by a parent, spouse, or other such significant person leaves unfinished business in both the physical and emotional realms. A sense of violation brings *indignation*; mistakes, *regret*; wrongful doings, *guilt*; and, damage to our person, resentment. Such accompanying emotions must eventually be experienced in order to complete closure, or else life continues to be interrupted by tensions caused by the resurfacing of the incompletion. This closure is a personal matter *mentally accomplished*, and may or may not require a reencounter with the original party involved.

Lack of completion, along with unexpressed emotions, causes a fracture in continuity—a separation, rather than fulfillment. Avoidance of what is set before us causes an abyss to be formed within awareness that interrupts the cycle of completion. Facing the painful situation and acknowledging such emotions helps to conclude the experience. Acknowledging human difficulties and their uncomfortable emotions requires vulnerability. Accepting vulnerability, and working through it with courage, builds inner strength. Paradoxically, the acceptance of vulnerability allows us to approach adversity with humility, rather than with the arrogance of an eternal combatant.

Holding another person or group responsible for maladies is a form of projection where attachment to blame or condemnation brings forth feelings of animosity, contempt, or hatred. Love is the polar opposite of hatred. Love identifies with others in a field of goodness rather than non-goodness. The traditional view of justice in our society is that when someone commits a bad deed, he or she deserves to be punished. The Western judicial punishment for crime and the mid-Eastern adage, "An eye for an eye, and a tooth for a tooth," perpetuate the cycle of discord. Here, the term *justice* actually means *revenge*. The human perspective views an external source as the cause of problems and responds with pragmatic laws and reprisals. However, condemning projections—demonstrations of our own internal conflicts—does little to address the causes within the Generative Principle.

Such judicial responses appear to enforce order in our society, but do not address the root cause of experience and *are of little help in resolving emotional predicaments*. Antipathy toward the *guilty culprit* and vindictive action of retribution avoids the messages from the Generative Principle and prolongs disharmony through the karmic cycle. Such attempts to combat symptoms ignore the causative kernel within the Generative Principle.

A similar principle applies to interacting with people having their own personal difficulties. Responding with *sympathy* to a person in pain or suffering, we feel emotional pain associated with *our* experience of *their* situation, *yet it is actually the pain we have within*. Sympathy is a natural, automatic response, representing a link of interdependency within human experience. Empathy, distinguished from sympathy, involves a deep understanding of another person's misfortune along with their emotion. Empathy need not result in sympathy; rather, empathy with compassion and a degree of equanimity, is a basis for constructively helping another.

Sympathetic emotions may have little relationship to others, and certainly do them no service. Deliberately cultivating sympathetic emotions is not especially recommended, although when such emotions spontaneously occur, erupting from the depths of subconsciousness, they deserve reception in awareness. Sympathy is a re-connection *with our own pain* through viewing the experience of another, thus providing another opportunity for resolving an incompletion within our own psyche. Another common emotion, *pity*, results from a *judgment* of another's misfortune. Demonstrating sorrow or pity for a person's situation can reinforce their self-pity in the dilemma, and further lead them to hopelessness and loss of self-esteem.

Situations invoke *negative attachment* when we either regret or feel guilty regarding our own past actions, or we resent the deeds of others. Such attachments, as the consequence of incompletion, can be resolved through forgiveness. A person's true being is eternal, instantaneous, continually renewed, and ever incorruptible. By releasing the past, we help clear the way for such spiritual qualities to be realized in earthly affairs. Although we cannot reverse the consequences of past occurrences, we can correct our view of worldly circumstances through the process of forgiveness, which is further discussed along with the technique of affirmative meditation.

Questions for Discussion

(1) In addition to anxiety, what fundamental value judgment and associated emotion is common to all other emotions of the Unfavorable World State?

(2) In what way do attachments of the Unfavorable World State mirror those of the Favorable World State?

(3) In human experience, are the judgments that range from good to non-good absolute measures, or are they subjective? Is there anything absolutely evil?

(4) What emotions are typically encountered in *approaching* a potentially threatening situation?

(5) What range of emotions occur as a threat is *encountered*?

(6) What possible emotions are associated with *separating from* a threat? Do these vary according to your selected action?

CHAPTER 10

AGONY OF DEPRESSED CONSCIOUSNESS

I knew a rather depressing young man who frequently proclaimed that *people are no good*. His experiences did not appear all that bad, but his perception of them was different. He seldom showed expressions of either joy or anger, and his energy level was minimal. His distorted viewpoint of external circumstances and restricted interaction likely resulted from a belief, such as *I am not OK* or *There is something wrong with me*. A bleak outlook and listless behavior represent typical symptoms of the State of Depressed Consciousness.

For various reasons, we often internalize difficulties of the external Unfavorable World, along with critical judgments and painful experiences, into our own self-identity. This outer-to-inner transformation contributes to the mental position of Depressed Consciousness forming a self-denunciation at the being level. As this evaluation is an obvious contradiction to spiritual identity, we can immediately conclude that Depressed Consciousness is *not* a natural condition. Nevertheless, this painful state into which we, humans, tend to slide is experientially real.

We devalue our conscious being, darkening our outlook with shades of black and grey. The most painful of emotions involving anguish, hopelessness, shame, depression, and immobilizing resignation are encountered in this state. All of these emotions interrelate to self-depreciation through the basic mental equivalent of I am not so good. In what way do they originate? Why are they maintained? And, how can we rid ourselves of them? We will address these questions in this chapter.

The conscious identification of *I am* is incorrectly associated with the self-evaluation of being bad. *Anger directed inward* is consequently a component of all emotions of Depressed Consciousness due to this erroneous evaluation. A common reason for this error is that adverse effects of the physical world are internalized rather than viewed objectively. Self-esteem is discounted as a consequence. Anger toward external objects diminishes and is replaced by internal anger that is felt as anguish, despair, or agony. This State of Depressed Consciousness with its self-depreciation produces the most miserable of human conditions. This mental pain has somatic counterparts ranging from a numbing of the senses to a feeling of *hurting all over*. Yet, this extreme level of discomfort sometimes becomes a catalyst for change, as it can range anywhere from self-destruction to a re-birth of spiritual awareness.

The voice of Ego erroneously assumes *I am in control of circumstances*. Inevitably, the Generative Principle asserts Her powers, disrupting the comfort zone, unbalancing our sense of efficacy, and leaving us deflated with feelings of inadequacy and helplessness. But, this shattered illusion of self-potency leaves an opening toward a greater, unseen power. Eventually, we come to realize that our achievements, which we embraced with pride as evidence of our personal competency, are but impermanent *gifts of grace*, the seasonal fruits of harvest. Then, we begin to move in concert with the Way of the Generative Principle.

Loss of Power through Change

As we become comfortably attached to a familiar environment, and depend upon it as a source of fulfillment, we become susceptible to material changes that inevitably occur with the potential of adversely affecting human self-identity. When *who we think we are* involves our own body and its environment, self-image can become disarrayed by events such as an accident, serious illness, breaking a relationship with a significant person, loss of a job, or the normal aging process. Even a positive change, such as the termination of an addictive behavior, may leave an unfilled gap in self-identity that produces a deflating effect. As altered relationships no longer conform to our conditioned expectation, we may feel alone and dejected, asking: *So, who am I now?*

If a person works for a long period of time to achieve a certain position or status, only to find that the position fails to provide or maintain the satisfaction so long anticipated, then he or she may experience disillusionment, with the resignation, *Is that all there is?* At this point, one may lapse into feelings of despair and bitterness. Whenever life's meaning and value are assigned to the projections of physical experience, the sense of wholeness is vulnerable to the mercurial changes of the universe.

Self-Blame

Self-condemnation underlies many conditions within Depressed Consciousness. Such self-blame originates either from our own judgment or is accepted as an introjection from someone else holding a position of authority. Often, roots of self-condemnation are implanted in our subconscious mind during the early formative years when we are more likely to acquiesce our right of discrimination to another. This surrogate authority might be an overly critical parent or abusive adult. It can also occur through intellectual subordination to the domination of religious dogma.

The religious concept of generic man being *born in sin*, for example, entails a righteous condemnation of the Human Self (pending salvation) to a never-ending punishment. This cruel and false myth, a doctrine of human denunciation contradictory to one's true spiritual nature, can be devastating to self-esteem and cause considerable and unnecessary guilt and anguish. This myth involves a concept of the Divine that is a throwback to the dominating, male divinity of past millennia, such as the ancient Solar God who ruled by fear, rather than love. The notion of feminine inferiority, dating from the Biblical creation myth, is likewise destructive to self-esteem.

By judging our circumstance within the physical world as being *non-good*, and transferring this condemnation to our being-level identity, we evoke the State of Depressed Consciousness. Invoking the *I am* at the being level, we then denounce ourselves as being bad, unworthy, imperfect, deficient, or damaged. If the resulting anger is not usually expressed overtly, it is experienced inwardly in a life of quiet desperation.

We feel at fault for things that go wrong, especially if they are sufficiently harmful, and have feelings of *regret* or *guilt*. And, if this guilt is internalized within our being level, we can be burdened with a feeling of shame, another Depressed Consciousness response. Shame is the emotion corresponding to transgression against our self-worth at the being level. Adopting the interpretation of John Bradshaw (1988, 17), guilt involves the opinion that I did something wrong whereas *shame* presumes *There is something wrong with me*. Guilt and *shame* correspond to assessments of our Human and Conscious Selves, respectively, as shown on the diagram below. A healthier way of reacting to negative experience is, for example, *I regret that have been selfish in my relationships, but realizing my mistakes and resolving to be more considerate, I will recover.*

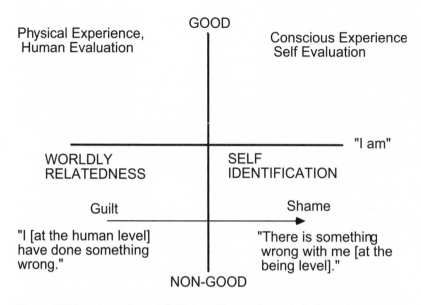

Figure 18. Transformation of Guilt into Shame through Self-condemnation

Ironically, there may be a sense of peace associated in the painful state of *depression*. Internalizing defects of the external world provides a sense of release from external turmoil. For instance, small children with abusive parents tend to assume that their suffering is due to their own fault, and thus discharge the distressing idea that their parents could be to blame.

A judgment of personal wrongdoing stems from an inner conflict with personal values or conscience that often originates from an external authority dictating what is right or moral. Seemingly harmless statements from family or peers can instill a belief that it is bad to display certain emotions. Anger exhibited by a child might provoke a verbal or physical reprimand, such as: *You're a bad child*, behave yourself! Physical or sexual abuse is certainly devastating to a child's sense of self-worth, where the humiliation often becomes transformed into more lasting shame.

Loss of Worth

Psychologists generally view *depression* as a *mood* affecting numerous emotions and feelings and having a constellation of symptoms. Yet, depression may also be identified as a recognizable emotion, a characteristic of the Depressed Consciousness State. When you say, *I feel depressed*, you are well aware of what you mean, however complicated the situation. Depression is a general emotion accompanying the judgment of *I'm not OK*. Through depression, we feel as though we have *lost a part of ourselves*, which results in the loss of joy, physical energy, or a zest for life. The combination of depression and other associated emotions, varying from person to person, combined with their physiological effects and projected experiences, constitutes the *mood* of depression.

Psychologists, through decades of empirical observation, have identified two types of depression: acute and chronic (e.g., Flach, 1974, 17-24). In the acute state, typically lasting from a few hours to weeks, a person is consciously aware of his or her feelings and emotional responses. People experiencing long-term, chronic depression often do not recognize their condition but, nevertheless, suffer from an affected worldly perspective with corresponding behavior. Some causes of depression are related to physical conditions, such as illness or body chemistry imbalances, and require supplemental medical attention in addition to the spiritual approach described below.

Depression, as a metaphor, is an emotional hole from which it is difficult to ascend. Through disenchantment with worldly experiences combined with a self-judgment of unworthiness, one becomes resigned to the futility of constructive action and self-nurturing. In feelings of helplessness and hopelessness, and with indifference toward the future, victims of depression are immobilized and frozen in their plight—with "walls of the hole" appearing unscaleable.

Despondency provides a desolate peacefulness of non-encounter; but this, too, is a form of depression, a dispirited condition where extreme loneliness pervades. A moderately depressed person might only procrastinate and appear to be bored or lazy. At other times, the behavior of one who is depressed is directly opposite to inaction, as if they are struggling against the chains of immobilization. It is the existing worthiness of the Spiritual Self that needs to be recognized and affirmed. A summary of thought and emotion of this state are shown in the figure below.

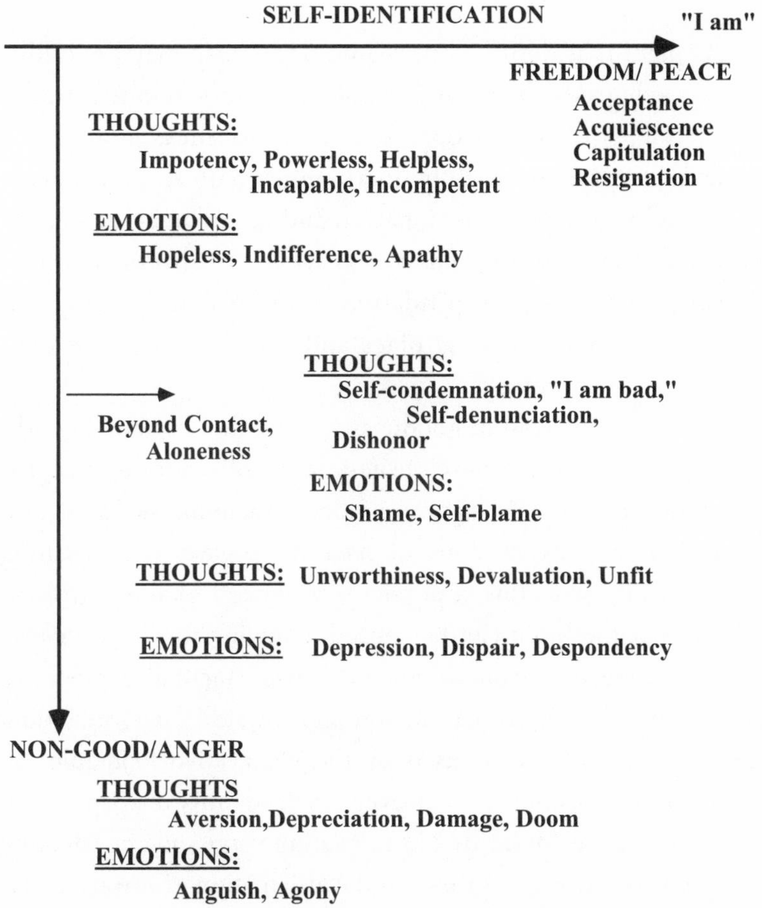

SELF-IDENTIFICATION   "I am"

FREEDOM/ PEACE

THOUGHTS:
Impotency, Powerless, Helpless,
Incapable, Incompetent

Acceptance
Acquiescence
Capitulation
Resignation

EMOTIONS:
Hopeless, Indifference, Apathy

THOUGHTS:
Self-condemnation, "I am bad,"
Self-denunciation,
Dishonor

Beyond Contact,
Aloneness

EMOTIONS:
Shame, Self-blame

THOUGHTS: Unworthiness, Devaluation, Unfit

EMOTIONS: Depression, Dispair, Despondency

NON-GOOD/ANGER
THOUGHTS
Aversion, Depreciation, Damage, Doom
EMOTIONS:
Anguish, Agony

Figure 19. Thoughts and Emotions of the Depressed Consciousness State

Mental and physical characteristics of the depressed mood can enforce feelings of impotency, which discounts the innate goodness of the Spiritual Self and disconnects from the potency of the Generative Principle. A retreat from external conflict provides no escape from internal pain. Rather, it can result in bleakness and despair. Perceptions of the environment darken so that life experiences appear to be seen through *muddy glasses*.

Recovery from the Depths

As painful as depression, shame or anguish may be, oddly, there is a degree of *peace* and *consolation* involved in the moods and feelings of the Depressed Consciousness State. The inward retreat from worldly fluctuations, with all their uncertainty and fears, brings resignation and compliance as a haven from external warring. The resignation of self-defeat offers appeasement through capitulation to outer conflicts, providing a psychological resting place and allowing space for consciousness to regroup.

The apparent void in goodness causing the dispirited condition of Depressed Consciousness also offers potential for reassessing identity. As nature abhors a vacuum, so Spirit also must find new expressions of itself to replace the resulting emptiness. Prior to this, a physician may need to apply medication so that the brain can be settled, allowing for a sufficiently clear consciousness from which a renewed spiritual perspective can be considered. Human action and physical laws, including medicine, are all means used by the Generative Principle. As consciousness becomes receptive, a self-identity incorporating goodness can be found by (1) reencountering and reevaluating physical projections, (2) through the affirmation of inward spiritual values, or better still (3) a combination of both.

For a shift in perspective to occur, leading to personal growth, one must again come in touch with discomfort and, propelled by pain, make a willful decision to know and accept a new identity and valuation for the Conscious Self. The first thing to be released is self-condemnation, best accomplished by forgiveness of both personal and projected transgressions. Forgiveness provides a cleansing and clearing, a conscious act soothing wounds of self-denunciation that allows the affirmation of inherent goodness.

Projections from a depressed state serve as a trap since they tend to substantiate negative beliefs by attributing them to external causes. But, projections can also provide new openings. Projections are the Generative Principle's way of offering a fresh, but difficult, opportunity to correct patterns of thought and feelings that originally led into hopelessness, shame, and depression. Through projection, that which has been repressed is eventually delivered forth again to objective awareness, the workplace of the conscious mind, where we can reencounter and reevaluate. This does not mean that all physical maladies encountered in the human experience can be corrected by conscious reevaluation. For example, natural events such as hurricanes, earthquakes, and contagious viruses—as products of the *World Soul* through Mother Nature—can trigger depression, either temporary or chronic. We all will eventually complete our human life cycle, and our loved ones may pass on before us; but, all experiences are necessary and appropriate in their time, however painful.

One pathway to the Spiritual Self, preferably traveled with a therapist or counselor, is to travel back through the human route of the Unfavorable and Favorable Worlds, back through adversity and rewards. In this way one may be able to dispel resistance, reclaim human powers, and aggressively pursue constructive goals that enforce a personal sense of achievement and value. Although this path may involve a long and difficult quest, the rewards provide a solid foundation for spiritual awareness. When goodness is internally realized, it will be demonstrated through manifestations, confirming and reinforcing positive beliefs. A danger involved in this approach is the temptation to assume that the human, egoistic self is responsible for the material successes achieved, rather than the Generative Principle. This is especially so in traversing the Favorable World State, though a pause in this state is certainly an improvement over depression. Also, with regard to making this journey with a therapist, counselor, or physician, worldly setbacks inevitably occur, discouraging one from the path unless support is at hand.

It is helpful to know that you are not alone in the process of regaining confidence and dignity. Therefore, surround yourself with supportive friends and professionals who will encourage and assist you along your journey and, most importantly, know that the power and intelligence of the Generative Principle will supplement your own efforts. As you begin to take steps, making decisions followed by personal action, unseen legions of natural forces will arise to assist you. Remember that you are never given more than you can handle, and that you are never without a pathway to recovery and finding your divinity within.

The direct approach to regaining your self-esteem is to know the true nature of your being, your Spiritual Self. As you come to know and believe in your fundamental goodness, the self-directed anger, depression, shame, and hopelessness will begin to dissolve, and a new outlook on life will manifest itself in your experiences. A most useful tool we will soon explore is that of affirmative meditation, an effective method for *preventing* depression and addressing its milder forms. The two approaches to recovery are illustrated below.

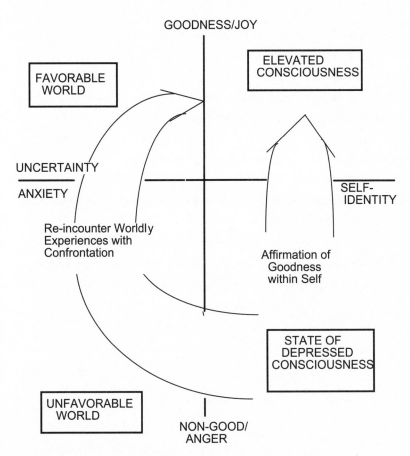

Figure 20. Two Pathways from Depressed to Elevated Consciousness

Questions for Discussion

(1) What changes in the fundamental judgments of *association* and *value* occur in the transformation from the Unfavorable World State to the Depressed Consciousness State?

(2) What effect does this transformation have regarding the emotion of anger?

(3) How do self-image and self-worth change in moving into a state of depressed consciousness?

(4) Discuss the transformation of *guilt* into *shame*.

(5) Why is medical attention sometimes needed in recovery from a state of depression?

(6) What are two pathways of consciousness that can be used in recovering from a state of depression?

CHAPTER 11

DEVELOPING MINDFULNESS

When it comes to your daily, Human Self activities, do you ever feel like you are steering a runaway car with no breaks, rolling down a winding mountain road where you stressfully react to unexpected sharp turns, and where the drama of experience totally commands your attention? Although you can steer your car to avoid a catastrophic collision, you cannot control how the road curves. Likewise, you cannot determine the pathway of your life. In the human dilemma, your awareness is often so locked upon the current drama that appears fatefully set before you that you continually view your circumstances through the clouded emotions of anxiety, hope, or fear. Under these conditions, it is very difficult to be aware of yourself as a conscious entity endowed with freedom and inherent goodness, or to realize peace and the joy of just being alive.

All of us have such rollercoaster experiences when we cannot attune to our true self. Even if one has been made aware of his or her spiritual nature, it can seem very remote and inaccessible during such times. As all earthly experiences come and go, another always occurs presenting a fresh opportunity to pause and reflect upon the nature of things. Rather than being a captive driver chained to a steering wheel, there are other options available through illumination of self-directed awareness.

There is an art and discipline to living in the world while being mindful of the Self as a free and wholesome entity. The endeavor of such living is something that can be progressively learned through dedication and practice. This *Way* is always progressive because it is open-ended and limitless. You may attain plateaus of heightened self-awareness, but there is always a higher level on the horizon, as well as a few ditches into which you occasionally will slip. It is the human condition that, as we achieve each and every step, another unexpected step is set before us projected from the depths of the Generative Principle. Sometimes we are successful, but other times we stumble. Yet, always, we have an opportunity to begin again.

Nourishing Nectar from the Wildflower Patch

For thousands of years people have used meditation as a process for training their minds. The primary difference among the many types of meditation is the object of attention. For example, the focus of attention can be simply the in-and-out movement of one's own breath. It might be sensory feelings within the body, such as the feeling of a chair or the floor, sensations of pain or pleasure, or feelings arising from emotions. Alternatively, the focus can be of a more external nature, as when attention is directed toward a sound, a flower, or a symbol. In addition, a mandala or mantra may have special meaning, resonating with inner concepts and values.

All of the types of meditation that I have encountered appear to be worthwhile in some manner. Each type meets the particular needs of some person or group, connecting with a personal or cultural orientation towards life. Despite cultural differences, human beings are all very much alike. As each wildflower in the field has its own substance and beauty to sensually and emotionally nourish, so does each of us when it comes to the spectrum of meditative practices. Most types of meditation direct attention away from daily activity, such as daydreams, anticipation of the future, recalling and reliving the past and, instead, *toward the present moment*. And, although this sounds like a simple requirement, it can be quite difficult, especially for a beginner.

Directing attention toward a particular object for an extended period of time is a discipline requiring practice. Some people train themselves with assistance from one of the many helpful texts, while others progress faster and better with an instructor. I explored numerous avenues of meditation with help from both classes and books before settling upon a practice that met my own needs. Participation in different types of meditation is enjoyable when the opportunity occurs. In the beginning, a decision and commitment to meditate is more important than selecting the technique.

Reasons for meditating are many, but relative to this book the primary purpose is that *applied meditation* can allow you to realize your spiritual nature. Realization is much more than intellectual knowing. It must be subjectively *experienced*. The intellectual principles of driving an automobile can be memorized from a manual, but no one can competently drive without practice. Attending to your spiritual nature is a pleasant experience that involves being filled with the emotions of peace and joy that enliven your existence. Dwelling upon such truths in a meditative state will alter your beliefs that, in turn, will change your outlook and experience. The benefits of meditation are not confined to the relatively brief periods you spend in practice, but extend to every aspect of existence. Your enhanced sense of self-worth will project outwardly and change the meaning and value of relationships with other people and events in your life.

The most common excuse for not meditating is the lack of time. The priority for finding the time is part of the commitment to practice. You *have* time, so the question is: *With what do you choose to fill it?* What are the real priorities of your life? Do they include finding your true nature and creating your own pathway, or are you too busy steering the runaway car? You *really are* free to choose. No earthly agenda supplants your conscious freedom. Even if you are not sure about embarking upon a journey of self-discovery, meditation has intermediate benefits. Just ease into it and see how it feels before making a life-changing commitment.

Meditation is often prescribed for stress relief. My barber, for example, related to me how meditation classes were part of his prescribed therapy following a heart attack. For many, meditation training is their first experience in learning to relax the body. But, more importantly, it also involves relaxing the mind. Much stress can be alleviated through meditation by releasing the anxiety of life's uncertainties. Activities of consciousness exist *only* in the here and now. Therefore, when meditation brings awareness to this changeless moment, anxiety-producing uncertainty is removed. The memory of this freedom from uncertainty is retained after meditation. As a fruit from the subconscious, it is carried over into subsequent worldly activities.

Although meditation originated in the ancient Eastern traditions of Hinduism, Buddhism, and Taoism, the techniques employed are just as relevant today. Some of the Eastern insights and terminology are appropriate for our understanding while we explore meditation as a means of Self-realization. For example, "mindfulness," a term from Buddhism, means to see things that are present with accuracy and full attention. During mindfulness, wandering of the mind is suspended, leaving the continual decision to remain focused upon what is at hand. Judging the value of things and experiences is particularly restrained. This mindful process of viewing things *as they are*, including one's own actions and reactions, is a cornerstone of Eastern meditation as well as its associated philosophy.

> Rather than anticipate the future, meditation can help
> you to come to know your present spiritual nature.
> You will discover joy in the journey as well as the
> unknown destination.

This practice allows you to release attachments, thus allowing the Generative Principle to accomplish whatever is appropriate according to Her schedule. You cannot be concerned about what will happen in the future while still remaining in the moment. *Desiring* a particular result was recognized by the Buddha as one of the *hindrances* to the pathway. To remain in the moment rather than in the past or future requires having no expectations, even regarding the benefits of meditation. So we are left with a paradox: if we do not anticipate an advantage gained from practice, why should we meditate? Meditation is for the present moment rather than for some future happening, and as this present moment is the only one that you ever know, why not enjoy it now. It is better to remain with *what is* in both external and internal experience, and release the rest to the Generative Principle.

How to Begin Meditating

Worldly experiences are so absorbing that we often get lost in the drama and forget that we have an independent conscious identity. Meditation is extremely useful in maintaining a perspective of conscious being. An initial step in meditation is to *create a space*, mentally and physically, conducive to this activity. The *intention* to meditate must come first, followed by a specific decision to begin that is accompanied by a priority to continue this activity instead of any other. My yoga instructor directs us to follow intention with attention. There are always distracting events competing for your attention, the psychic momentum from unresolved, resistant bodily sensations such as fatigue or hunger, disquieting sounds from barking dogs, or anticipation of an unwelcome interruption. This is an occasion for constructive suppression. It can be helpful to imagine a volume control on your senses and turn it down. These distractions then become secondary to your intention to meditate.

Choose a physical space where you can escape intrusion, minimize distraction, and feel more comfortable and secure. Eventually, you may be able to meditate at most any place and time, but initially it is better to find silence and seclusion. When at home, I use a room upstairs where I normally study and write. Here, I feel comfortable because it is *my space*, or as much as any space on earth can be.

Attend to your physical body so that it can be comfortable, passive, and minimally distracted during your meditation. *Sitting* with straight spine is the generally recommended posture. The prone position is more likely to produce drowsiness, but it may be appropriate for certain occasions. Yoga classes, for example, finish with *savasana*, or corpse pose, where each person lies in a relaxed, yet awake, meditative state.

Begin by relaxing your body. You may not realize that your body is tense until you pause to observe it, so the following routine may be helpful. Focus upon an extremity of your body, such as your lower legs and feet, deliberately tensing and then relaxing. Proceed to your upper legs, advance through your abdomen, chest, arms, neck, face, and even your head. Alternately tensing and relaxing creates an observable contrast, training your body to recognize the relaxation sensation.

Meditation involves a *controlled directing of awareness*. For that reason, the relaxation procedure, itself, represents a preliminary type of meditation. *Concentration*, useful to the meditative practice, *is the discipline of maintaining attention*. The mind must be trained to concentrate for each separate application. Just as a basketball player concentrates upon the rhythm of the game, yet may not be able to transfer that ability to other activities such as working math problems without specific training, meditation requires training. Meditation involves a sustained concentration upon a chosen object or activity preferably having a meaningful relationship to the observing, subjective self.

A good meditative exercise for beginners is that of *observing the breath*. After relaxing your body, shift your focus to the movement of your breath. Simply follow the cycle of inhaling and exhaling, continuing as long as you like. Breath-watching involves the rhythm of your body and will engage your attention, directing it away from daily concerns. Breath has always been associated with life and vitality. "Life-breath" is a translation of the Sanskrit word *prana* from the ancient Vedic texts—where breathing practices were believed important in the development of the individual into the Atman or Supreme One. A relevant purpose of *pranjama*, yogic breathing exercises, is to re-vitalize the participant.

Breathing is a metaphor for the entire human experience through the understanding that it can be either voluntary or involuntary. You can assume an active role in conducting the affairs of your life, or you can remain passive and allow the Generative Principle to create the unfolding experiences for you; even when you forget to breathe, the Generative Principle continues for you through your involuntary nervous system. You will find it easier to relax and release unto the Generative Principle as this becomes clearer.

March of the Monkey Mind

After relaxing your body and quieting the senses, direct your attention internally rather than upon external objects. Begin with a procedure called *thought watching*, where you simply observe the emergence of thoughts and emotions as they arrive. Releasing attachment, allow them to dissipate like mist rising from a pond. Alternatively, turn your attention to the empty space between thoughts and expand this emptiness. Acknowledge and respect the content of your awareness as it arises. It is important *not to resist* thoughts and emotions because this engages the mind in negative attachment rather than freeing it to be an objective observer. Avoid the diversions of fantasy, letting such temptations pass. Know that you may at any time resume your usual activities, while also realizing that you are free to continue your meditation.

Freedom cannot exist without options, and you have innumerable options for awareness—so many, in fact, that you may feel inundated by distractions. But, rather than becoming perplexed by this vast array, rejoice in freedom! Then apply discernment to this freedom of decision. Otherwise, your mind will be like a feather blown around in a turbulent wind. Simply observing, rather than reacting, will provide you with stability and peace that is obtainable in no other way.

When you sit to meditate, it may seem that there are a thousand voices in your head screaming for your attention. Some call this *mind chatter*. Ancient masters from the East referred to it as the *monkey mind*. This influx of distractions can seem very demanding, insisting you march to its step. With such thoughts and imagery filling your awareness, it can be difficult to recognize your own independence.

Descartes' declaration, "I think, therefore I am," is misleading. Although thoughts allow us to become aware of our being,
they do not *define it*. Thinking is only an activity of your conscious
being. The conscious activity of thinking is a *sufficient* condition
for recognizing your *I am* being, but it is neither the only nor the
necessary condition, for there are other conscious activities that
can so inform you. A more proper statement would be, *I am,
therefore I can think*. You are a conscious entity having awareness,
with or without thoughts. Stepping outside the framework of
thought and imagery, you realize that you are the host of your
dwelling, and that random thought or sensual distractions are but
guests subject to your forbearance. It is not necessary to drive
them from your house for, as unruly as they seem, they can do
you no harm. Observe them objectively as from a vantage point
and, when you are ready, politely release them to leave. You are
the master of your own attention.

The Color of Emotions

There are times in the life of every person when their emotions
or moods become so dominant in awareness that it is very difficult,
if not impossible, to disengage and maintain mindfulness. When the
Generative Principle's messages become this assertive, it is time to
stop, listen, and respond. If you have a flat tire on your car, it must
be changed before you can proceed, and this same principle applies
when you are emotionally incapacitated. Your activities continue to
be compromised if some action is not taken.

Although we are spiritual beings, we cannot forever remain
in a state of bliss while dwelling in our human forms. Meditation
is not just about achieving and maintaining a special state of consciousness, because all such conditions are temporary. Mindful
meditation is also about being open and receptive to life experi-

ences as they arise from the Generative Principle. Your preference may be to select those blissful encounters most representative of your Spiritual Self, but if that is not the Generative Principle's current agenda, then first attend to what is at hand.

Working through a difficult emotional situation can be an occasion of increased understanding and personal growth. If significant emotional problems exist during attempts of meditation, disturbing the concentration of attention that is the very heart of this practice, it is better to directly address difficulties rather than circumscribe them. Some people attempt to escape emotional encounters by submerging themselves in work, sports, TV, drugs, or alcohol. They refrain from inner psychic activities such as meditation just so that they can avoid facing their difficulties. *I just can't seem to concentrate*, they say. But the unspoken, and often unrealized, message is: *I wish to avoid encountering my emotions*.

Meditation is a way of being in the now, and that is exactly where emotions are found. Some emotions are painful and their encounter may involve suffering. No one enjoys suffering, yet engagement is often necessary in order to affect a resolution and to move beyond it. An aspect of meditation is to be open to *what is*, and if emotional discomfort is the dominant experience, then reception is in order. Rather than seeing emotional occurrences as disruptions to meditation, it is sometimes better to incorporate them as a special part of meditation.

That which appears as a blockage can also be the doorway to a breakthrough. Emotional *hang-ups*, as they sometimes are called, are usually such doorways. Your freedom will increase when you have worked through and beyond emotional interruptions. Disturbing emotions are expressions of subconscious beliefs contrary to your spiritual essence and, thus, form blockages to realizing your true nature. Blockages may include any of the emotions or associated moods as were described in all the States of

Conscious Evaluation outside of Elevated Consciousness. The Buddha identified five hindrances to the spiritual journey. Consisting of emotions and behaviors, these hindrances are personified by "Mara the Tempter" in Eastern mythology. The five hindrances are exemplary of difficulties encountered in meditation and are identified within the structure of the States of Conscious Evaluation, illustrating (Figure 21) the utility of this perspective.

The five hindrances of Buddha are desire, aversion, laziness, restlessness, and doubt (as expressed by Goldstein and Kornfield, 1987, 31-45). Note that these five characteristics are common to all of us to some degree. Yet, they may not be hindrances unless they are so intense that they interfere with directing attention. If we note their presence and lightly dismiss them, they are but additional mind chatter. However, if they become dominant in conscious awareness, then it is better to encounter them rather than to suppress them.

The first two, desire and aversion, are polar emotions resulting, respectively, from positive attachment in the Favorable World and negative attachment in the Unfavorable World. Underlying *desire* is the idea that something *out there* is good for me and needed to fulfill myself—it is *apart* from me and I feel deficient without it. Ego desires this object and pictures it as a necessary source of personal gratification. For example, one may long for a relationship with another person, a particular possession, advancement of social status, or just a box of chocolates.

If you know that you really want a new car, it is a simple matter to work toward that goal. But, *desiring* the car may mask deeper roots of discontent that are more complex and hidden from your awareness. You may crave something unidentified, beyond your immediate knowledge. If, for instance, as an infant your family did not have sufficient food and you were always wanting, you may now be seeking a nebulous source of security.

Your human needs are quite real and need not be denied. But, a new car may only temporarily quench your craving for security. Permanent security at the being level will come only with realization of your spiritual nature.

Eventually you will gain insight into the underlying thoughts, ideas and value judgments that generate the emotion or feeling. These indicate the root conditions of the emotion that compose the cognitive equivalent of the subconscious kernel. This kernel is buried within unconsciousness and is not directly accessible. Yet, emotions will be indicators assisting in deducing the cognitive equivalent by utilizing the States of Conscious Evaluation as previously described.

Once the cognitive equivalent is determined, you can reexamine your original evaluation relative to your current perspective and personal values. Your previous evaluation was formulated at another time, under circumstances involving different purposes and values, and prior to your present objective of knowing your Spiritual Self. Your personal values were likely influenced by the standards of others, possibly those of your parents, but you can now realize the pain resulting from prior decisions. If the cognitive equivalent is *I feel insecure*, then you will benefit by meditating upon the permanent goodness, freedom, and invulnerability of your Spiritual Self. This inner fulfillment will help provide a conscious haven from worldly threats.

Making new evaluations allows you to replace old cognitive equivalents with new ones. For deep-seated emotional difficulties, this procedure may involve considerable time and dedicated effort, but results will be worth it. The assistance of an experienced counselor or therapist can guide you in such matters, supplementing your meditation practice. Yet, no one but you can do the important work of reevaluation and re-decision. Only new evaluations can result in more pleasant emotional responses as these will be the heart-level confirmations of your new cognitive equivalent.

The second hindrance, *aversion*, is an emotion based upon the idea that some person, circumstance, or event in an Unfavorable World threatens your goodness and peace of mind. Associated emotions include fear, anger, hate, resentment, or sadness. Here, I might perceive some adversary as depriving me of something I need, preventing me from accomplishing a goal or threatening harm. Adversarial issues include an illness or accident, change in social or financial conditions, competition in business or romance, or a physical or verbal assailant. The Human Self is negatively attached to such opposing forces through struggle, an adversarial linkage that produces discomfort. Ways of resolving adversity include confrontation, forgiveness, removing one's self from the circumstances, or reexamining the tribulation to determine if the event is really a threat or merely an element of passing change.

Laziness, the third hindrance, is sometimes a symptom of apathy characterized by a lack of motivation and vitality. Laziness must be distinguished from fatigue and sleepiness, both of which have physiological similarities, with rest or sleep being remedies for the latter two conditions. If you feel tired or sleepy, but want to meditate, splash some cold water on your face, and sit in a firm, upright chair. Laziness is a behavior that often finds a peace through resignation toward remaining in a powerless state of disinterest.

At other times laziness stems from issues of diminished self-esteem and is a behavioral characteristic of the State of Depressed Consciousness. This mental attitude typically results from a belief in personal *incapability* or *invalidation*. This immobilization supports a *safe position* that doesn't risk failure, but forfeits any possible benefit of constructive action. You might think, *It is not worth the effort to find anything better, so why try*, or *I am not worthy of finding peace and happiness, so this path is not for me.* The human organism tends to act and move toward compensating benefits. The *action of inaction* through laziness clings to a dubious status quo that allows one to escape the fear of futility or failure. Here, either the pain is not great enough or the vision of reward is not clear enough to provide motivation. Since the Generative Principle does not support such a position, Nature's pendulum will swing either toward pain or prize, making inaction an intolerable choice.

Restlessness, the fourth hindrance, is a physiological effect and behavior that is a near opposite of laziness. Restlessness agitates the mind and body. Like a barefooted child jumping along on a hot pavement, the mind jumps from one possibility to another without focus. Indecision thus pervades and consciousness is confused by the multitude of worldly uncertainties and complexities.

Anxiety, an emotion underlying restlessness, vacillates between hope and fear. Bringing the attention to the here and now, away from the unknowable possibilities of another time and place, is a remedy for both restlessness and anxiety. Slow down the mind by gently focusing upon something having movement and dependable rhythm, such as your breath. Through patience and compassion, agitation will begin to dissipate. If anxiety is due to a more severe experience such as traumatic stress, it may be advisable to limit your initial meditations to a few minutes at a time.

The last of the five hindrances is *doubt*, which occurs when hope is diluted and one looks downward into the negative possibilities of human existence. One might question: *What if the materialists are right and my mind is nothing but a bunch of nerve cells firing their electrical discharges in a deterministic manner? What if I have no free will and my destiny is predetermined?* But, doubt also stimulates inquiry that may clear space for creative possibilities. You encounter an eternal, uplifting essence as inquiry is directed inward toward the Spiritual Self. There you find an internal substance that weathers the storms of uncertainty.

Draw forth the truth of being from the wellspring of the Generative Principle, which brings peace and fulfillment that transcends doubt. Such an experience is very personal and cannot be borrowed from another. Emerson says it well: "Meantime, whilst the doors of the temple stand open, night and day, before every man, and the oracles of this truth never cease, it is guarded by one stern condition; this, namely: It is an intuition [as a cognitive encounter]. It cannot be received second hand" (Dillaway, 1990, 45). Lasting faith is built upon *subjective* engagements with truth, rather than what is read or received from external authority. This faith is enforced by internally experiencing successes with spiritual self-discovery while confronting doubt. Thus, hindrances have been called *manure for enlightenment*—with doubt providing especially fertile soil.

As you begin to know your Spiritual Self through explorations of consciousness, life's eternal values and essence-of-being are unveiled, contradicting those kernels that bring forth hindrances. The eternal values of Elevated Consciousness offset and counteract those of other states. When hindrances arise, you have alternative choices upon which to base new judgments that untie the ropes of world dependency in which you have been bound. This does not mean that hindrances can be totally eliminated, although they will diminish in frequency and intensity. Hindrances, like dark clouds, occasionally will arise. But, through the ascending perspective of your Spiritual Self, you can be aware of the light behind the clouds. The five hindrances are illustrated on the next page, showing how they relate to the States of Evaluation.

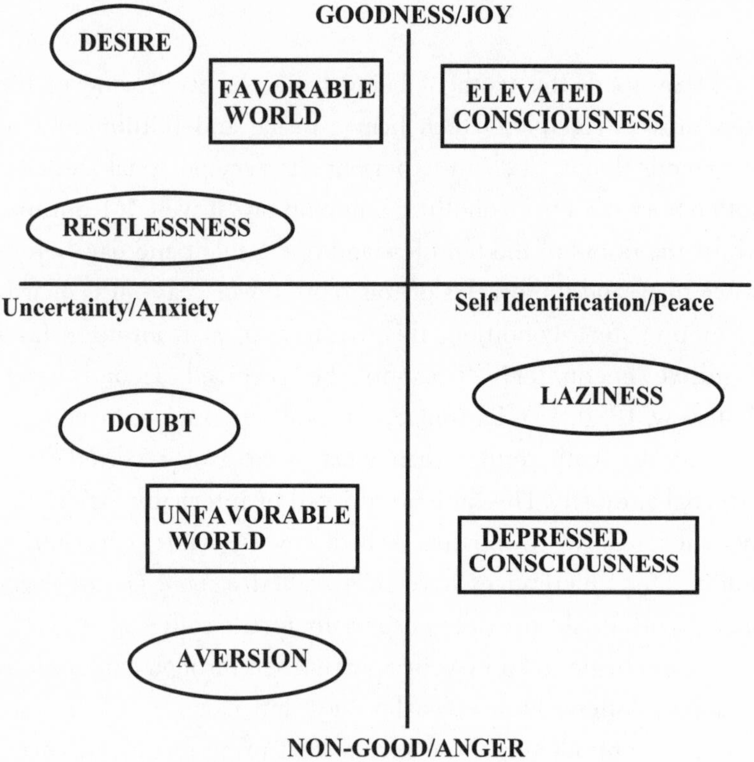

GOODNESS/JOY

DESIRE

FAVORABLE
WORLD

ELEVATED
CONSCIOUSNESS

RESTLESSNESS

Uncertainty/Anxiety   Self Identification/Peace

LAZINESS

DOUBT

UNFAVORABLE
WORLD

DEPRESSED
CONSCIOUSNESS

AVERSION

NON-GOOD/ANGER

**Figure 21. The Five Hindrances Relative to the
States of Conscious Evaluation**

Questions for Discussion

(1) What are the benefits of meditation?

(2) What is required to begin meditating effectively?

(3) How can you deal with thoughts that interrupt your meditation?

(4) How does shifting your attention to your spiritual identity
assist in clearing your mind of distractions?

CHAPTER 12

THE ENCOUNTER
OF YOUR LIFE

Life at the Contact Boundary

Being in the *here and now* delivers the mind from all anxiety. Here, we do not wonder what is happening back at the office or what another person might be doing. We release the curiosities about tomorrow and remembrances of the past. This is the *contact* boundary, previously introduced, where the *space is here* and the *time is now*. Here, we experience the message of the Generative Principle and openly encounter physical existence. What you will have for dinner tonight will not be a consideration when fully engaged with the immediate. The contact boundary is where non-material consciousness, itself unconditioned, meets worldly circumstances as they now exist, without reflection upon causes or conditions external to the immediate experience. The boundary is the meeting place of two perspectives, one in which you are the subjective observer and the other as an objective participant. Being present at the contact boundary is to be fully attentive, alive, and expressive. Employ your physical senses and direct your attention among aspects of experience and interaction.

Intimacy always exists at the contact boundary where there is no separation between subject and object for these, intertwined as experience, live existentially within your awareness. Such intimacy allows you to be fully present with other people, hear their words, and see the expression on their faces. Intimacy exists whether the relationship is in harmony or conflict. At the contact boundary, interaction is spontaneous and immediate because you cannot rehearse words while remaining in the moment.

There is no lack of expression at the contact boundary for it continually flows from that endless wellspring of life. Your actions, in word and deed, are more creative because you resonate with spontaneous manifestations and immediate emotions. With your heart and emotions guiding you, the Generative Principle responds to your reception, facilitating creative responses as you dwell at the contact boundary. Spontaneous emotions can occur ranging from joy to anger these being *immediate* emotions delivered along with experience as discussed in Chapter 6. Thanksgiving is a specific application of joy, indicating that you acknowledge an experiential blessing. Surprise and enjoyment are other immediate responses as you encounter goodness, whereas painful encounters might produce shock, anger, or even horror.

If you experience desire toward an object, then you have disconnected from the contact boundary, and you are picturing the object as separate from your needy Ego Self. You no longer appreciate it as it is, but rather view it for what good or harm it can bring to you. Fear indicates that you are looking toward the future possibilities of distress. Sadness or resentment both revert to remembrances of past experiences outside the moment that were previously painful. Anxiety, hope, and doubt refer to uncertainty that is far from the concrete present. Remaining at the contact boundary requires a continuous decision to do so. It is easy for the mind to deviate from the physical and internal psychic reality of the moment and step into the world of abstraction.

There is nothing wrong with leaving the here and now, and to anticipate what is likely to happen. We accomplish many useful things by lapsing into thought, especially if it is disciplined and controlled. But, even though visualization and memory recall are important functions of the human mind, they are no substitute for spending time in the moment. In an imagined space and time, using imagery, we *think about* how we should respond to the situation rather than acting spontaneously.

Breaking contact with the immediate environment and withdrawing from it is sometimes necessary. Some forms of contact are not in your best interest. For example, escaping from danger, avoiding an energy-draining relationship, and attending to other matters of importance or interest are all good reasons to disengage. Yet, when contact is appropriate, it can be a most rewarding activity. As stated by Fritz Perls: "The man who can live in concernful contact with his society, neither being swallowed up by it nor withdrawing from it completely, is the well integrated man...He is the man who recognizes the contact boundary between himself and his society, who renders unto Caesar the things that are Caesar's and retains for himself those things which are his own," (1976, 26).

The contact boundary is a meeting place where you can commune with nature or really get to know and understand another person. Life is not static. You can paint a landscape, conduct a conversation, make love, or play an intensive sport while being totally present. Certainly, the situation is not totally without thoughts but they, too, can be immediate and relevant to the moment.

Just ask mountain climbers what they *think about* while scaling a vertical granite wall. Their attention is fixed upon the task at hand: *Is this handhold secure enough to support my weight? Can I remain balanced while I extend my leg to reach that foothold?* Why do they stay focused upon the here and now? They have intent, that is, a motivation driving their continual concentration and pure engagement with the present environment. Their very survival depends upon it. Remaining in the moment requires concentration and discipline. Life at the contact boundary is a continual exercise in freedom as one always has the option to deviate from the here and now and venture into the there or then. These decisions require careful balance in choosing to focus upon the present instead of the numerous options.

Poised in Freedom

Moving inside the contact boundary and attending to your conscious entity provides a different option. This Conscious Self is distinct from your Human Self, with whom you identify through your body, work, physical relationships, and all the other worldly trappings. How do you make this step from observing the world into awareness of *pure consciousness*? It becomes easier with practice. Try this simple exercise: Close your eyes and ask yourself: *What shall I think of next?* There, in this brief moment of reflection, you are aware of your awareness and choices in pure consciousness. It's just that easy to become "conscious of being conscious." Maintain this practice by continuing to know that you are in command. *Freedom of awareness* is a primary attribute of consciousness with *choice* as the field in which freedom plays, as illustrated below. From the vantage point of conscious freedom, you can look outward into empirical imagery of physical associations, or inward into the internal aspects of your own self, while still employing basic judgments of quality, association, and acceptance. You are an important participant in the life process as you augment this freedom of consciousness with personal action.

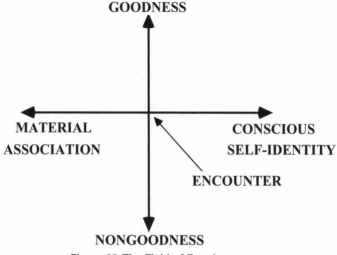

Figure 22. The Field of Freedom

When you are absorbed in earthly drama or fantasy, swept along like a cork bobbing in a stream, you lose your conscious efficacy, your vantage point of freedom, and no longer serve as the masculine God. From the worldly outlook, prejudiced by material attachments, something might appear to be a necessity, while from freedom's unlimited perspective it is only a possibility. Some restrictive bounds appear when the Human Self is entangled with material conditions but, in contrast to this conscious freedom, conscious mind maintains a state of *freedom* only by distinguishing itself from its human identity, i.e., practicing detachment.

Non-attachment is not the same as *indifference*. For example, the physician in the hospital's emergency ward must be relatively objective and detached from the trauma experienced by his patients in order to perform his work. Yet, he is not indifferent to their pain and suffering. Instead, the physician balances awareness of his patient's pain with the healing effect of his treatment. Indifference, in comparison, is either a callousness that tromps upon caring and feeling, or is a withdrawal from awareness. The field of freedom is obstructed through indifference because choices of awareness become narrowed. A temporary peace may be found while retreating into indifference, but it is a "peace of extinction" rather than aliveness. The full experience of life requires a courageous meeting of both pain and pleasure; that is, engaging the intimacy of life but disengaging from attachment to it. As Ego attempts to possess experience, it becomes either a boon or burden, leaving emptiness upon its departure. The Conscious Self views not only the phenomenon of experience, but also its impermanency and fleetingness.

In Harmony with Uncertainty

As previously mentioned it is impossible to continually remain in the moment; because the Generative Principle paints worldly experiences with the pallet of time and space, She provides tempting pathways that lead beyond immediacy. When you wonder about *what is next* or *over there* beyond the present experience, uncertainty occurs. Beyond the contact boundary, events are viewed with some sense of separation and with emotional shades of anxiety. You never actually travel to the past or future, but rather you only imagine it in the present. In this *here and now* you invoke an emotional involvement with the actors of your imaginary play. You dread a business meeting tomorrow that never happens exactly as you pictured it. Awareness of the Conscious Self provides grounding in the moment and, if appropriate, allows you to objectively view the past and future as present-moment constructs in imagination.

When the two perspectives—the subjective observer and its external object—are seen apart-yet-together, an emotional transformation can occur. Most religions explore a concept of *oneness*, but a particularly relevant view comes from the East. Ray Grigg in his *The Tao of Zen* discusses oneness with the insightful observation: "Closeness and distance are opposites. So are oneness and separation (1994, 224). Later, while commenting upon Kapleau's statement "The truth is that everything is One, and this of course is not a numerical one." Grigg continues: "This One is a sense of unity that includes all separation" (1994, 225).

These phrases may merely appear to be additions to the many cherished paradoxes of Zen and Taoism, but meaningful interpretation can be given by examining this terminology within our graphical model in Figure 23. Introducing the Western concept of consciousness validates these intuitive truths and removes the paradox. Being close to an object in the sense of being fully attentive to it, yet maintaining an identity separate from it, constitutes a type of unity. For example, one can feel unified with another person through being attentive to that person. Bringing an object to the immediacy of the contact boundary invokes the *intimacy of encounter*. This is unification in consciousness rather than in space, and allows the observer to become one with the multiplicity, yet not a numerical one.

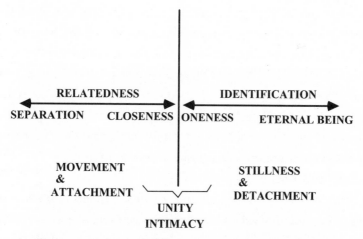

Figure 23. Intimacy of Encounter at the Contact Boundary

This intimacy requires strength of self-identification that is neither dependent upon, nor totally attached to, the object. Any association involving attachment relates to the Human Self, a relationship potentially unstable. Self-identity grounded in consciousness detaches from this variability, thereby maintaining stability. The Generative Principle's expression within the external world, including imagery of past and future, is observed with peace and harmony from a stance of the immovable, changeless being. Unity between the inner and outer occurs in such an encounter of the here and now.

As self-identity with pure consciousness grows, so does a sense of unity. *Real life is conscious life*, and in consciousness we are all free, equal, and united. Realizing and accepting the universal identity of all individuals as *conscious beings*, while invoking the decision of acceptance, unveils the natural linkage of *love* as the ultimate, unifying principle. An incorporation of all other life emerges through this realization and unites all as a collective one.

The uniqueness of each individual does not dissolve in this realization of oneness. Differentiation, as seen from the grounded Conscious Self, is only another facet of awareness upon the gemstone of oneness. This correlates with an analogy from ancient India where, in the Net of Gems, each gem reflects all others (Campbell, 1988, 111). You are my projection and I am yours. The infinite variety of life requires uniqueness through this separateness of individuals. Closeness and distance are opposites only in perspective. Their union is not otherwise contradictory. All life is unified in spirit, but displays unlimited diversity through freedom and expression.

Shunryu Suzuki wrote in his *Zen Mind, Beginner's Mind*: "Our usual understanding of life is dualistic: you and I, this and that, good and bad. But actually these discriminations are themselves the awareness of the universal [material] existence" (1973, 29). Therein, Suzuki identified the two types of opposites: *association*, the "you and I," and *quality*, the "good and bad," both of which are needed to describe the broad perspectives of "universal" human existence. These opposites can be observed in this book as polarities upon the graphical structure of Conscious Evaluation. The *field of freedom* requires this distinction of contrasting options relative to association, quality, and acceptance. This simultaneous existence of reverse counterparts, recognized in Taoism as well as Zen, may be termed the *balance of opposites*. Where there is no distinction of choice, there is no freedom. As Suzuki expressed it: "To try to obtain freedom without being aware of the rules means nothing" (1973, 34). Again, choice is the ground upon which freedom plays.

In order to appreciate the quality of experience, the full spectrum of goodness must be seen. That is, if an event is seen to be favorable, what characteristics made it appear so in contrast to the unfavorable alternatives? For a situation viewed as unpleasant, what attributes would make it more enjoyable? There can be no sense of magnitude unless this range of possibilities is considered.

Ancient Chinese wisdom recognized the interplay of positive and negative aspects of the universe through the diagram of T'ai-ki, as pictured below, incorporating all opposites (for example, day and night, life and death, good and bad, truth and falsity, beauty and ugliness, or mountain and lake). The Yang and Yin, representing the positive and negative, are respectively shown in the diagram as the white background with a black spot and black background with a white spot. They are likened unto two intertwining waves of air and water, with a drop of water in the air and a bubble of air in the water. The two opposites are united in a dynamic, interactive balance. Both are enclosed in a circle symbolizing the unifying and creative principle, the Tao.

Figure 24. T'ai-ki Diagram of Balanced Opposites

It is significant that all of the opposites represented by the T'ai-ki diagram are spatial and temporal manifestations of the universe. We encounter contrasting differences of physical reality through experience and imagination—with opposites analogous to a Newton Law of Motion stating that every force is met with an equal force in the opposite direction.

Conscious balance is a mental poise in attending to your current options. You maintain balance while remaining in the present at the contact boundary. Here, the Human Self engages in earthly joys, aversions and anxieties, while the Conscious Self watches without attachment. Both *hopes* and *fears* may be observed as consciousness looks over the shoulder of Ego without judgment, but with great interest. Remember that Ego is not really an entity separate from consciousness, but is only a different perspective whose reference is from the human body. It is important not to create an artificial dualism between the two since they are merely alternative orientations of awareness. Ego watches the world, while Conscious Self watches the watcher.

To release egoistic attachments to the world is analogous with the Biblical injunction to *die unto the world*. Acknowledge the earthly passions of your Human Self, but in meditation patiently let them dissipate, returning to present awareness. In this way, you can be master of your awareness, so that all potential objects of attention are subordinate to your volition. As a corollary in deference to the Generative Principle, no one can truly be master of anything *except* his or her own attention and mental action. You are a master to the degree in which you assume control of your consciousness.

Equanimity is an objective perspective that recognizes gratification and suffering, but is liberated from attachment. This detachment allows you to observe from a balanced position that is grounded in the reality of conscious being, i.e., being aware of your own changelessness in the swirl of impermanence. Equanimity involves an understanding and empathy for the perpetual changes within human experience. It acknowledges and respects the unique pathway that the Generative Principle has delivered to each individual for personal growth, providing an opening from which spiritual love, compassion, peace, and composure can arise. The perspective of equanimity provides a good posture to begin your meditative practice. The following section summarizes the steps described above that lead to this position.

The Spectrum of Awareness

Along the pathway of developing mindfulness, numerous mental postures are encountered. Prior to achieving focus, the mind responds with emotions and conditioned behaviors, *automatically* reacting to unfolding circumstances rather than to conscious decision. Lacking self-determination, awareness is like a feather blowing in the wind, its identity intermingling with the swirl of surrounding events. But as you assume conscious control and focus your attention, response becomes more deliberate.

The six steps itemized below progressively lead away from anxiety and toward freedom of consciousness. In Figure 25, these steps are illustrated as points along the axis-of-association within the States of Conscious Evaluation. Begin your path toward mindfulness by viewing worldly experience objectively as an array of options. Know that there is *nothing you have to do*, and that you are free to choose among unlimited possibilities.

1. Focus your attention, freeing yourself from distractions and realizing that such self-discipline is a choice you are free to make.

2. Come to know your own body, attending to the physical sensations, actions (such as breathing), feelings, and emotions that accompany experience. Learn to recognize various emotions as they occur, noting the underlying thoughts. Spend some time getting to know your self in human form.

3. Be present in the here and now, while still knowing that recalling the past, speculating about the future, or wandering in the realm of fantasy are all options of your mind. Choose, instead, the option of remaining completely within the moment in contact with immediate manifestations. Truly encounter your experience on a one-to-one basis at the contact boundary.

4. Know that you, the conscious observer, are distinct from all material objects of your awareness. Recognize that you are an independent operator selecting the focus for your attention. You are a stationary and separate point-

of reference of the eternal moment around which moves the ever-changing, which is continually unfolding from the Generative Principle. Practice this perspective of just being aware as a conscious observer.

5. Distinguish between the uncertainties of worldly fluctuations and the unchanging nature of yourself as an observer. Feel the grounding of yourself within each eternal moment. Suspend all judgments, seeing yourself poised in the freedom and balance of your own independent decisions. Allow yourself to enjoy the peace that naturally comes from this perspective and your autonomous capability.

6. Declare your identity in an invocation, such as: *I am a spiritual being, free in consciousness.* After developing comfort in this position, you may proceed with an additional step leading into *affirmative meditation* such as: *I am whole, complete, and secure within my being and am peacefully linked with others through a natural connection of love. I am thankful in this realization.*

It is important to realize that mindfulness is not a state at which you arrive and remain. Rather, it is a path upon which you tread back and forth, purposefully interacting with the multitude of life experiences. There is no single way to live. Creation is too varied to prescribe such a static position. Tread along this path of mindfulness that encompasses the spectrum of possible associations with experience. Interest and aliveness will be your reward.

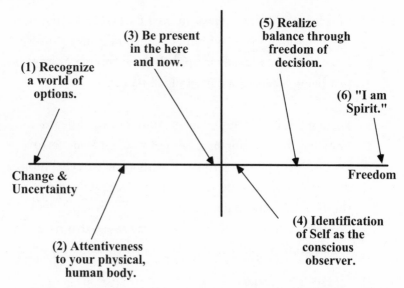

Figure 25. Pathway of Mindfulness through Association and Identity

Questions for Discussion

(1) Describe the encounter described as the *contact boundary*. Why is it referred to as being *intimate*?

(2) Explain the difference between *non-attachment* and *indifference*.Can you feel unified and intimate, with a sense of oneness, with your experience without being attached to it?

(3) Why does equanimity and wholeness necessitate embracing the duality of *good* and *bad*, and *you* and *I*?

(4) How does embracing a sense of *oneness-with-others* relate to the connection of *love*?

CHAPTER 13

AFFIRMATIVE MEDITATION

The Mental Setting

Would you choose to be a perfect statue carved from ice and safely displayed away from the maddening crowd in an arctic wasteland? Probably not! Such an existence would be very boring, indeed, and not at all fulfilling. Yet, *there* you would be a beautiful creature, an example of artistry and goodness with no opportunity for mistakes. Instead, you are human, warm with rich emotions, consciously painting your experience with tonal shadings ranging from good to bad. You can mess things up or you can make things better.

You are free to choose and, together with the Generative Principle, design your earthly experience. You, alone, fashion your self-identity. Relative to yourself as a conscious being, you have two choices regarding quality: self-affirmation or self-condemnation. As shown in Figure 26, you may judge, *I am good* or *I am bad*. However, evaluating yourself as *bad* at the being level is an error, allowable in freedom of judgment but contrary to your true nature. Goodness is the true nature of your conscious being, the character of your Spiritual Self. Yet, the Generative Principle responds to your beliefs about yourself, rather than to this true nature. When you criticize yourself because achievements do not measure up to arbitrary human standards, you malign your Human Self, and likely transfer this attitude to your Conscious

Self. In response, the Generative Principle provides confirming experiences corresponding to such judgments.

You came into this world with a conscious mind characterized by goodness and freedom. Evaluations to the contrary may sometimes enter your thoughts, but they do not change your basic nature. Erroneous ideas cannot lodge in consciousness because it has no storage mechanism. But, if not challenged by personal values, erroneous ideas can be transferred to memory within subconscious mind and, subsequently, influence experience.

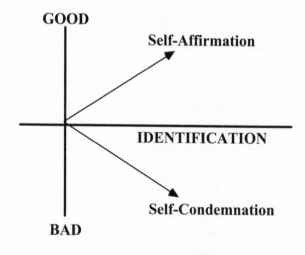

Figure 26. Possible Quality-Judgments Regarding Your Conscious Self

Practicing Affirmative Meditation

Developing mindfulness provides meaning and presence to your experience through greater awareness of the world around you, as well as awareness of yourself as a conscious being. Most significantly, mindfulness clears space, allowing further discovery of your own spiritual nature.

Many practice meditation strictly as a passive activity, with this seeming to be particularly true in the East where it originated. To actively guide the mind is a turn to the West. Active meditation commonly includes *guided meditation* employing imagery. In this book, another form of active meditation is *affirmative meditation* that embraces specific positive values. In affirmative meditation, one's *self-consciousness* is first distinguished from the physical body and its environment. It is this consciousness of being conscious that receives the affirmation. Affirmative meditation is distinct from positive *thinking*, which is sometimes used to affirm the imminence of some event desired by the Human Self, but disregards the agenda of the Generative Principle.

Most of us enter meditation from the hectic environment of the material world and require some time to ease tension and agitation. I often begin by moving through the steps of mindfulness as described Chapter 11, while avoiding being caught up at any particular phase. In a quiet, comfortable space I first acknowledge the events commanding my attention and the effect they are producing in my physical body. Since these feelings correspond to my emotions, I just allow them to be. If I am distracted by sounds or other external sensations, I recognize them and permit them to fade away in my awareness. I see myself as an entity observing present-moment events with an option to shift my attention away from them. Identifying myself as a detached, objective observer is necessary so that I am not overwhelmed by limitations of the physical world.

As long as you are caught in the tribulations of a human identity, you cannot completely embrace your natural goodness. You are still a human, but you are also much more than that.

Affirming Your Spirituality

Affirmative meditation is an active path upon which you direct your awareness toward your spiritual nature. Here, with gentle firmness, you take charge of your mind and attend to the truth of your being, utilizing the unbounded freedom of your conscious nature and exercising will and autonomy. This is your individual responsibility, a most important task that no one else can do for you. Identify the quality of your unique existence and honor that flame which burns only within you. This is an important endeavor for your spiritual realization. You might begin with something similar to the following:

> I affirm my freedom of consciousness and proclaim goodness to be the quality of my nature. In this moment, I know that my conscious nature is pure and clear, running strong like fresh spring water from an inexhaustible source. I realize that goodness is eternally available at every instant and, therefore, my being is whole and complete with nothing lacking to be added, and with nothing excessive or impaired to be removed.

As simple as this may sound, it is not always easy to voice such affirmations with enough conviction to impact the kernels within subconscious mind and affect manifestations. How can you realize the degree of your convictions? The best indicators are *arising emotions*, for they are your experiential confirmation. Joy, springing from realization of goodness, is indicative that you are convinced of your essential self-worth. Joy is the natural emotion arising from an encounter with goodness, so open yourself to receive and appreciate its presence. Know that you deserve this joy. Since your essence is goodness, joy is your spiritual heritage.

The greatest obstacle in realizing the goodness of your Spiritual Self is a mistaken identification with your egoistic self. You have previously looked upon apparent human limitations and imperfections, and allowed this material self-image to blend with that of your conscious being. It is difficult, but necessary, to release this human view and look afresh at the *real* you. Refuting *that which is not* may be a necessary conscious exercise prior to the process of affirmation. You may, for example, literally *tell yourself* that your Spiritual Self is not affected by what you have done, what you possess or lack, what other people think of you, or even what you previously thought of yourself. Here, you are not denying the human, physical world, but rather you are making a distinction between it and your Conscious Self, one that is born anew with wonder and innocence at each moment. Following this conscious discourse, your actual meditations directed to your subconscious need to be an affirmation, rather than a negation. You may acknowledge and affirm:

> *I am now speaking as a spiritual being of pure consciousness where I have no past or future, but just am. I rejoice in the essence of my being which I recognize and accept as being unconditionally good.*

Spontaneous affirmations, spoken from the heart, are recommended over those given by rote. Memorized affirmations lack the creative spark of present-moment examination and qualification. Religious liturgy, hymns or chants repeated mechanically, for example, will have negligible impact upon the Generative Principle. Your memory within the Generative Principle is the origin of these recollections, and thereby you are creating nothing new. Such repetitious activities may help bring you into a spiritual mood in preparation for meditation, but to serve as creator and change your experience, you must create. That which is freshly created within consciousness is empowered to produce a greater generative effect. When consciousness abdicates its freedom of choice, it becomes bored and apathetic. Creativity is exercised and empowered as consciousness assumes the responsibility of directing its contents of thought. Do not concern yourself greatly with the specific words of your affirmation, for *intentions* will carry the import.

Creativity begins in your conscious mind, which then initiates all manifestations through the intermediary of the Generative Principle. She provides the fiddle, so to speak, while you must compose and play the tune using the infinite variety of notes available. You are both free and capable of composing the *music of the spheres*, arranging the notes in the manner most pleasing to you. You do not need an external authority telling you how to compose your affirmations or live your life! In this endeavor you need only allow natural goodness to flow from the center of your own being in any of its multiple forms.

Since spontaneity is characteristic of your natural, creative being, your composition will improve with practice. But, though you are intrinsically free to direct your attention, you are continually being lured toward the trappings of the external world and personal habit. In one sense, this freedom is as effortless as sliding on ice, but ice *skating* requires developing skill. Remaining in the moment allows spontaneity and, like ice skating, it necessitates the practice of continual choice and deliberate motion.

The Healing Effect of Affirmation

There is wisdom in the saying that *to solve a problem, go where the problem is not*. When you have a material problem, identify with your Spiritual Self, which has no problems. Your spiritual nature is always accessible with a shift of attention, allowing return to peace and harmony. It's just that simple, but as mentioned previously, simple is not always easy. Affirmations of your inherent goodness provide a correction of contradictory subconscious content, replacing seeds from which spring unpleasant weeds within your experiences. Even so, the only way to obtain a more satisfying and fulfilling experience is to change false underlying beliefs.

Sincere affirmations of the truth of your spiritual nature effortlessly refute the negative evaluation of life. There is no conflict involved in making this correction because, as a movement in consciousness, such freedom knows no obstacles. What is, as realized truth, *excludes that which is not*, i.e., that which is an error. The Eastern expression *enlightenment* is appropriate here because truth excluding error in consciousness is analogous to a beam of light shining into and dissipating darkness. Error, like darkness, does not consist of any substance with which to resist truth. However, identifying and unseating error deeply embedded in the subconscious may require numerous conscious affirmations.

The Generative Principle's manifestation of new kernels, founded upon affirmations, are *always* perfectly accomplished, but through Her infinite and impersonal wisdom She decides the how, where, and when. To expect specific worldly demonstrations, as *you* consider appropriate, is usually a formula for disappointment. Furthermore, such expectations entail attachment to particular forms of goodness with an associated anxiety toward attainment. Goodness is a far more general principal than can be evidenced by any preconceived expression. Trust in the Generative Principle to deliver the best for each moment. Just let go and let the wisdom of the Generative Principle manifest.

"To everything there is a season," and therefore *all things shall pass* is true for bad experiences, except that they also tend to return again in modified form unless a mental correction is made. The healing of any painful situation requires a change of perspective. Only by altering underlying kernels of belief can permanent healing be obtained. Affirmative meditation targets "culprit ideas" embodied in kernels of belief and, thereby, contradicts the erroneous cognitive equivalents that produce unfavorable manifestations. In determining the cognitive equivalent to be addressed, the emotions of the experience are indicative of the underlying value judgments composing the kernel. The kernel reveals itself through its signature, i.e., those telltale immediate emotions accompanying the experience.

Consider a person who feels economically insecure, with the dread of poverty always lurking. Through constant fear, any accumulation of material wealth or position by this person is viewed only as a *defense against loss*. Appreciation of comfort is undermined by the apprehension of deprivation. Adversarial forces continually appear to deplete existing reserves, so that life is seen as a struggle. Here, the fear of poverty is the immediate emotion indicative of the kernel to be addressed.

I'm just trying to keep my head above water is the figurative expression referring to an apprehension of debt where the flood of financial obligations lap against the hip pocket. One is reminded of a non-swimmer fallen into a lake, frantically thrashing to keep his head high and fearfully gasping mouthfuls of air. In contrast is the experienced swimmer who lays his head onto the support of water and efficiently propels forward, knowing that he can gently roll around to inhale from the inexhaustible supply of air. In this same way, you can trust in the Generative Principle, relax unto Her, and rely upon Her inexhaustible provision for your needs. It is much easier to form such trust when you realize that goodness is your birthright in spirit and, like the trained swimmer, you are capable and *worthy* of receiving your due rewards through your sacred union with the Generative Principle. An affirmative meditation addressing economic insecurity could be as follows:

> *I now turn within and affirm my true nature. I am a spiritual being recognizing goodness as the unrivaled quality of existence. I am endowed with freedom to dwell with this realization, knowing that in spirit I am whole and complete, lacking nothing. I prosper in this life-sustaining abundance, rejoicing with a feeling of thanksgiving. I am secure in knowing that the Generative Principle continually provides the best opportunity for growth leading to the earthly demonstration of my spiritual goodness.*

Such an affirmation can assist in countering experiences of lack and deficiency, yet it is more powerful when the confirming emotions of joy and thanksgiving accompany thoughts. The act of formulating and repeating the affirmation is a systematic means of employing your rationale, but the transformation of these ideas into beliefs can be blocked if the emotions that naturally accompany such ideas are not also accepted and embraced. Sometimes positive emotions relating to personal happiness are rejected because they contradict closely held beliefs in unworthiness, and are typically accompanied by guilt, resentment, or fear.

Consequently, some cling to a painful human identity enforced by subconscious kernels, and refuse to accept the spiritual identity rationally affirmed. *Words and ideas may lead, but confirming emotions must follow.*

I once knew a man who was very intelligent and highly trained in practical, academic terms as well as in philosophies of the spirit, but who continually felt unprosperous. Although he knew how to formulate wonderful affirmations, he absolutely refused to permit himself the emotional expression of joy, thanksgiving, or peace *prior* to some material evidence of worldly manifestations. The happiness of attainment always appeared beyond his reach. As the chicken laying infertile eggs will never view its offspring, you likewise must allow and appreciate the fecundity of joy, peace, and thanksgiving in order for your affirmations to be productive.

Consciously celebrate the realizations of goodness that occur in affirmative meditation. The dialectic formation of affirmations based upon your spiritual nature is important, as some structure and logic within your affirmations are necessary in order to focus your thoughts toward the truth of your being and away from worldly circumstances. But, good meditations require emotional as well as verbal content, for such uplifting emotions are confirming echoes of truth given to us by the Generative Principle.

When you turn attention inward for meditation, thoughts frequently turn to pending events of the day. Realize that you can either follow this train of worldly imagery, or you can choose to attune to your own conscious nature. Acknowledge your conscious choices and see them arrayed before you for selection. Affirm that you are in control, and then focus upon your freedom of decision. Find the *peace of the decision maker, a peace in the security of conscious control.*

Peace is more than a word or a thought, for it also represents emotion and feeling. Words are useful in providing thought with a structure in forming affirmations, but words forever remain abstractions of the thing, itself. We never know a flower by *thinking* the word *flower*, but rather we must see and experience it *as it is*. And so it is with peace, an emotion of harmony that must be *felt*. We can use words to construct affirmations for meditation, but we need to move beyond them to find inner meaning.

Turn toward your own essential quality and appreciate its goodness. Know that you exist in momentary consciousness and nothing external can affect this excellence. Dwell upon this self-evaluation of goodness, responding to it with joy. Know that all aspects of life in spirit are associated with goodness, and receive them with the feeling of thanksgiving. Look beyond to other spiritual beings surrounding and uniting with you. Recognize the goodness in others and embrace it with acceptance through the feeling of love. Such affirmative meditations are a celebration of life and, though they are not directed toward specific worldly situations, they are instrumental in therapeutically manifesting general well-being.

Why Not Prayer?

In our Western civilization, *praying* is the more common approach for improving situations through conscious means. So, why not discuss prayer, rather than affirmative meditation? And, is there a difference? People pray in many different ways, so prayer and affirmation can be similar. *Affirmative prayer*, for example, is similar to affirmative meditation.

Dr. Larry Dossey in his books, such as *Healing Words* (1993, 169-195), describes scientific experiments that have shown notably, yet inconsistently, the effectiveness of prayer in healing medical conditions. Generally, unspecified in these experiments was *how the participants were to pray*. A variety of religious faiths and philosophical orientations were represented, so the method of prayer was not uniform.

The common ingredients of prayer found effective in healing are attitudes of empathy, compassion, an intent that *goodness shall prevail*, and belief in *powers beyond the self*. Such elements affect subconscious beliefs in a positive and beneficial way, so why not pray? Prayer can be extremely valuable, but it is also important to do so with awareness and understanding of the process involved.

Synonyms offered by the dictionary for the word *pray* include: entreat, supplicate, implore, beseech, and petition. The Latin root for prayer, *precari*, is translated as *to beg*. Traditionally, prayer is viewed as a supplementary process for filling a deficiency or to correct a wrong. The one who prays in this manner, therefore, identifies with the human condition of incompletion and separation from goodness. This person typically appeals to an external source of supply, such as God or a Supreme Being, to intercede by divine intervention, to provide or rectify. As such, prayers appear at times to go unanswered. The inference is that this external source chooses with discretion to either grant or withhold the sought-after goodness.

In contrast, affirmative meditation seeks not externally for goodness, but looks within to the essential spiritual nature, affirming *what is* rather than *what might be*. The source of physical manifestation is recognized as lying beyond one's self and the realization that each person is *always connected with goodness at the being level*. Every being is empowered with efficacy in consciousness, where the power and intelligence for explicit corporeal demonstration is attributed to the Generative Principle. No specific manifestation is sought through affirmative meditation but, instead, an identification with the wholeness which always is.

Affirmation of one's spiritual nature, viewed as a prayer, is *always answered*, for spiritual nature is eternal, needing only to be recognized. This realization provides a healing of mental conceptions and displaces erroneous assumptions.

The difference between a prayer of supplication and affirmative meditation is a judgment in association of the *self* relative to goodness—*I am separated from goodness*, in contrast to *I identify with goodness*, as shown graphically in Figure 27. Prayers of supplication represent the perspective of the isolated human identity expressing hope, whereas affirmative meditation portrays the integrated Spiritual Self. Prayer, as such, is an activity practiced in association with the Human Self, while affirmative meditation *unites with spiritual identity*, graphically represented by the State of Elevated Consciousness.

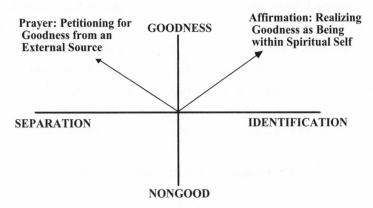

Figure 27. Comparing Prayer and Affirmations as Polarities of Association

Prayer incorporating *hope* supports the belief that there is a *possibility* that goodness will occur. Implicit in *hope* is also the belief that goodness *might not* manifest in a probabilistic world of uncertainty and anxiety. The belief that prayer *may not* be answered establishes through the Generative Principle a material likelihood that *it will not*.

With affirmative meditation, specific manifestations from the Generative Principle cannot be anticipated. This point emphasizes another important difference: whereas prayer implies an attachment to the physical occurrence of goodness in order for fulfillment to be realized, affirmative meditation realizes wholeness independent of manifestation. An external God does not "tweak the universe" by responding judiciously to prayers that interfere with nature. Rather, the universe responds like an echo from the divine ground of being in accord with natural order.

Affirmative meditation is a wonderful approach when one is able to use it. But, there are times when human conditions make it very difficult to realize internal peace and goodness due to painful circumstances. Until the body and mind can be stabilized, an interim approach is to utilize methods of the Twelve Step programs, beginning with "I, of myself, can do nothing." Yet we know that we are instrumental in creating, along with the Generative Principle, a better experience using the tools of prayer or meditation. Both prayer and affirmative meditation also invoke a version of the second of the Twelve Steps, "I rely upon a power greater than myself [as Generative Principle] to restore (the human condition)."

Affirmations for Healing Others

Can affirmative meditation heal the problems of others? Perhaps we can assist, but first it is most important to realize that *what appears* in our experience of their misfortune is a manifestation of our subconscious, whereas *their experience* of the same events may be quite different. Our pain may have no relation to another's feelings. It may be difficult at times to realize this distressing fact. We can only be responsible for and affect our own beliefs and experiences. While we may desire to be helpful to others, we must be aware and respectful of their freedom of will beyond our control, a sacred aspect of each person. There are appropriate circumstances where we may override the will of other people, such as in correcting the behavior of children or incarcerating dangerous criminals. Yet, in efforts to *help* others with pain or problems, it is seldom necessary to impose our will over theirs.

When you are aware that someone wants change, this provides a good opportunity for affirmative meditation. Certainly, you never know the subconscious content causing their physical dilemma, or whether their desire for change includes altering beliefs, yet a potential occurs for assisting them. As you bring people into your awareness, acknowledging their maladies and empathizing with their condition, your image of them is only another projection from your own subconscious mind. The subsequent mental work involves your own thoughts, which in turn affects only your subconscious mind and experience. Your task is to heal *your vision* of them.

The aphorism, "You can't love someone else, unless you love yourself," is applicable to the use of affirmative meditation for the benefit of others because it is highly advisable that you become well-grounded in your own spiritual identity before intentionally addressing other people's problems. Use caution while engaging in other people's situations, remaining clear about your own spiritual identity and its qualities. Before you undertake a meditation regarding another's painful situation, develop a state of mindfulness regarding your own self-worth and freedom of consciousness, as well as the goodness of your own nature, and the independence of this nature in regard to any other person's predicament. Whatever result follows your meditation, know that you are secure as a spiritual being, relying upon the power and intelligence of the Generative Principle. If an outcome does not correspond to your ideal, know that you are not responsible for the personal demonstrations of others. Continue to realize their spiritual nature independent of physical manifestations.

On the positive side, a part of you is healed as you realize the spiritual nature of a troubled individual. Visualizing another person from a spiritual perspective, you are complying with the ancient Greek imperative: "Physician, heal thyself!" In *The Road Less Traveled*, Dr. M. Scott Peck states: "Again, as I look back on my successful cases, there is not one that did not result in some very meaningful, often radical, change in my attitudes and perspectives," (1979, 149). In general, the *only way* in which difficulties can be corrected is through a change in belief.

If you engage in the process of affirmative meditation regarding another person, yet they are not ready to alter *their* beliefs, is the process then in vain? Meditation is always effective for *your* consciousness. As a result, your experience of the other person will change. Affirmative meditation is performed *about* someone rather than *for* someone. In the most profound sense, you alone cannot help anyone. Although you may appear as part of the process, others must also help themselves. The sole purpose of meditation regarding others is to see them as spiritual entities, rather than human. That experience is sufficient for both you and them. A physical, synchronistic change may occur, or it may not. Your meditation concerns their spiritual identity. It holds no attachment regarding what the Generative Principle shall manifest, as *that is* Her prerogative.

Individuals who are the subject of your meditation may have either a remarkable recovery, remain the same, or even die. However, the chances of their recovery are better because of your meditation. Double-blind studies employing prayer, in the referenced book by Larry Dossey, confirm this statistically. Prayers or meditation are more effective when they are requested, as the request invokes hope and expectation regarding powers beyond themselves. Their willingness and receptivity affects the physical *possibility* of change.

There is a definite linkage between all persons within the Generative Principle, specifically within that which we term *subconscious mind*. As there is One Generative Principle, there is also *one subconscious mind*, wherein we each have a store of individual beliefs in addition to shared collective beliefs. This is the reason why we can share a common world where all personal experiences are perfectly synchronized and coordinated according to individual belief. The Generative Principle also contains the *control center*, so to speak, that responds to this one universal, subconscious mind. Within the Generative Principle, there are many facilitating sub-principles and interconnections bearing fruit in response to the affirmation process. This realm of the Generative Principle may forever remain beyond our understanding, yet we can witness how compassion and love through meditation and prayer have their effect upon others who are consciously receptive.

Forgiveness

Major obstacles in forming effective affirmations result from the condemnations of our self or others. If such denunciations appear to be rationally substantiated by material standards, we may be reluctant to forgive another or ourselves, believing it would be a travesty of *worldly justice*. Through judicial standards, we tend to hold physical cause-and-effect relationships inviolable, with compassion withheld and considered inappropriate for those facing the consequences of their own actions. Though there may be some validity in the pragmatic philosophy of *tough love*—which allows people to learn from and suffer for their mistakes in order for them to grow in self-reliance—as an alternate perspective, we can know and pursue the transcending idea of grace through affirming the spiritual reality of all life.

Forgiveness mentally overturns prior condemnation, reversing the conviction that someone has done something bad, deserving retribution. Condemnation is an attachment to a negative experience, as in: *He did something bad, and thereby he deserves my resentment and anger.* But through condemnation, who is in pain? The person responsible for the transgression may experience pain as a consequence of his or her action, but my personal condemnation produces pain felt only within myself and results in *my* experience of an Unfavorable World.

Condemnation often results from righteous indignation toward the perpetrator of some misdeed. I might rationalize, for example, that *I have a right to condemn them and to be angry about what they did.* True, but I have a *right* only in the sense that I have the *freedom* to adopt this conscious judgment and negative feeling, rather than a positive one. Conversely, I also have the freedom to release mental condemnation and resentment with no compromise of worldly justice.

Forgiveness does not absolve another person's misdeed. Rather, it is a *process of freeing oneself* of an unnecessary mental burden. If another person has willfully acted to harm someone, there is a system of balance in the universe—some call it *Karma*—where the Generative Principle has Her means of compensation beyond our understanding. Our act of forgiveness may not affect this process, yet it does affect the quality of *our* experience. Forgiveness is more difficult when our projection involves a person we dislike. But, why should we bond through the attachment of animosity to someone we find unpleasant? Forgiveness can be seen as a release from this painful bondage where we, *shaking the dust from our feet*, are freed to follow our path, and they theirs. It is easier to forgive if we understand that it is also for our benefit.

Other people, as they appear in our projections, have a special metaphorical relationship to us. When, through condemnation, I judge a projected shadow figure as being wrong and deserving of my indignation, I feel this anger within. Of course, it is difficult to see this shadow as an aspect of myself, although when I can, I am more likely to respond with understanding and compassion. Sustained anger can precede many internal physical conditions, such as heart attacks and ulcers. As all worldly experience is a projection of what is within, emotions assigned *externally* to our shadow have an *internal*, reciprocal effect; that is, they are one in the same. Holding animosity toward our projections causes a blockage to our own healing. Self-healing occurs as we forgive our shadow as a projection of ourselves. This psychological truth underlies the message of Jesus that *we are forgiven as we forgive*. The interpretation of Jesus' phrase by some Christians is that forgiveness comes from an external God or from some representative authority in the Church, but the position of this book is that forgiveness comes not by an external power, but from within.

Giving up condemnation relieves emotional pain. Forgiveness is simply the giving up of negative attachment that, in turn, allows an emotional release. Self-forgiveness is also important, in that forgiving oneself means to forgo self-blame, guilt, and regret. Although prior actions may result in a harmful consequence, the concept of sin as a metaphysical blemish on the judicial creative powers is a fictitious idea. We cannot change the past, but we can release our negative attachment to it. *Forgive and forget* we are told. And, the order is important because to forget *prior* to forgiving is an act of suppression, perpetuating the cycle of adversity. Forgiveness involves the *assimilation of experience* rather than its rejection. Whereas rejection is a form of incompletion, release through forgiveness is a form of graceful completion and closure.

Personal Action: The Dance of Life

There is a time to meditate, and then a time to act. Your capacity for physical action is essential for your earthly demonstrations and is *integral* to the creative process of the Generative Principle. She creates your personal experience, often requiring your active participation. Your human experience is a dance of life in which you move as partner of the Generative Principle. Your part is relatively easy requiring only one step at a time, although the choreography may appear complex.

How, you may ask, can I completely rely upon the Generative Principle, but also act decisively in taking responsibility for my life? Your first line of responsibility is in thought, followed by action. Recall that most spiritual masters, such as Jesus and Buddha, were quite humble in their worldly actions. Remaining humble while acting decisively is not a contradiction, for such is the divine balance in reverence to the Generative Principle. The best that we can do is to act conscientiously with the best of intentions, attending to that which we envision as being good.

Determination toward a goal, while realizing physical uncertainties, requires courage of conviction. Although such determination does not insure success, people who repeatedly try are more apt to achieve objectives. Accomplishment is more likely as we persist with both *conviction* and *expectation* of success. Convictions certainly contribute to the mobilization of personal effort. Perhaps, more importantly, they *augment* subconscious

belief and activate forces of the Generative Principle. Our subconscious may have unknown contents that impede our efforts,
but persistent convictions with right purpose tend to dissolve
obstructing beliefs. Repeated human effort chips away at physical blockages, increasing the likelihood of desired results.

Acting through Inner Security

As you come to know yourself as a spiritual being, attending
to present-moment existence, you become aware of the eternal
goodness of your nature, *independent* of worldly outcomes, and
observe events with an inner security. In spirit, you are a rock of
permanency surrounded by a sea with waves of impermanency.
Events forever come and go, but you remain unchanged in your
spiritual nature. All experience is useful and relevant to your pathway, so relax and appreciate the game of life you play with the
Generative Principle. Know that She does not play against you but,
instead, acts as a facilitator and companion.

When in doubt regarding proper action, just *try something* that
appears to lead toward your objective. One of my most important
lessons in college occurred when a math professor put a difficult
problem on the chalkboard, completely baffling the class. As he
demonstrated one particular solution, I asked: "How would we
know in advance how to do that?" His simple response was: "You
must just *try* something." Thereafter, I noted that if I only *thought*
about a problem, seldom did I envision a solution. But, when I
took pencil in hand and began to *try something*, the solution usually began to unfold. Soon I began to realize that this was good
advice for all endeavors. The very intention to obtain favorable
results activates forces of the universe. When you *move*, every particle in the cosmos resonates in accord through the same powers

of the Generative Principle that animate your body. There appears to be a universal intelligence that is activated as you move.

Mistakes guide you and provide new direction because unsuccessful attempts to achieve desired results eliminate approaches you need not try again. Many such trials are often required for success, just as repetitive attempts are often needed in a learning process. Just ask any professional basketball player how many times he missed the hoop in developing his skill. Corrections and adjustments along your successful path require flexibility and frequent re-decision. Flexibility does not mean that you are uncommitted; rather, a continual evaluation and response is needed as developments unfold. The essence of your vitality is *conscious efficacy*, the realization that you are not chained to prior, inappropriate decisions. You live anew in liberation each instant as you respond to each experience.

Purpose and Destiny

Is there a purpose to life? We might feel morally or religiously compelled to find some positive, uplifting answers relating to perfection, enlightenment, or blissful nirvana. But, as freedom of will is a most sacred and inviolate characteristic of individual consciousness, then what type of externally imposed, preordained purpose could possibly supersede any personally selected intention? The Generative Principle has no agenda other than manifesting those kernels deposited within subconscious mind, most of which are unknown to you. Any single, absolute purpose of human destiny would be contradictory to freedom of will. Life for the individual and society will be generally enhanced as each person willfully discovers his or her spiritual identity. A viable demonstration for human existence is to exercise conscious freedom, expressing personal goodness through creativity. Greater fulfillment will be realized by connecting with others through the natural linkage of love; but this, too, is subject to individual decision. Reality and value can be found in each precious moment, recognizing and appreciating the significance of today.

You do have a current pathway that might appear as destiny, but the pathway is subordinate to your freedom in evaluating each encounter and choosing the next step. In the absence of absolute purpose, what remains upon which to base decision and action? Such is the dilemma of the masculine God incarnate, but it is also the palette for creativity. As people become aware of their spiritual nature, the more likely the world will evolve with a society embracing peace and harmony.

The Wonderful World of Serendipity

As you plant seeds within your subconscious mind, you can be assured that they will bear fruit within your experience, even though the particular form and occurrence remains unknown to you. As you work toward specific goals, the Generative Principle's vision for the appropriate experience may be different from yours. Know that goodness is a quality appearing in innumerable forms, and that during the unfolding of your life, you will always encounter things that surprise and delight you. This is the *principle of serendipity*, which assures that unexpected forms of goodness will occur in your experience as a manifestation of the seeds you plant. The act of anticipating serendipity, in itself, is effectively a form of affirmative meditation.

Pursue your personal goals realizing that you will progress, but do so without attachment to the final configuration. Anticipation of serendipity is similar to the childhood game where a friend hides, then suddenly jumps out for your amusement and pleasure.

Appreciation of serendipity does not come automatically. You must be alert and observant to recognize the varieties of goodness, otherwise you might be disappointed that specific expectations are not realized. As a child playing hide-and-seek expects to be surprised, *expecting unexpected goodness* will enliven you.

Become as a child expecting serendipity, for then the uncertainty of the Generative Principle's beneficent manifestations will lend excitement to your life. Such is the positive side of anxiety, where the unpredictability of worldly events is welcomed with energy, interest, and gratitude. Adapting the phrase from the book of Mark (10: 15), receive the kingdom of goodness as a little child; else you may miss it through the myopic vision of human expectations.

Questions for Discussion

(1) What are two possible quality judgments regarding yourself as a conscious being?

(2) In forming affirmations, what indicators provide confirmation of your level of conviction?

(3) Why is it important to spontaneously compose your affirmations rather than use those memorized or read?

(4) If affirmed *truth* effortlessly excludes *error* in consciousness, why does the correction of experience sometimes require time?

(5) Why do affirmations need to be made with no expectation of specific results?

(6) What favorable emotions are likely to occur in the process of affirmative meditation?

(7) What are typical similarities and differences between affirmative meditation and traditional prayer?

(8) What are the possibilities and limitations in using affirmative meditation for addressing the problems of other persons?

(9) How does forgiveness remove blockages to effective affirmations? How does personal action augment and support your affirmations? How do you allow for serendipity in your expectations?

CHAPTER 14

FROM MYTH
TO REALITY

It is helpful to review the long path we have traveled in discovering inner divinity, and how you may interact with the Generative Principle in creating a better life experience. We examined the archetypical basis of the Generative Principle as reflected in the early myths and practices of early civilizations, increasing in sophistication through the millennia. Next, we further explored the foundation of a philosophy identifying the New Trinity as individual consciousness interacting with the Generative Principle in forming phenomenal manifestations. This involves a psychology of the non-material, individual conscious identity existing only in the moment. We learned, by way of a model of thought, judgments, and corresponding emotions, how to develop mindfulness and practice affirmative meditation. We now recapitulate the steps along this pathway and summarize our conclusions.

Generative Principle through Mythology

Allegorical representations of the Goddess from past millennia are helpful in forming a metaphorical perspective of our interactive role with the Generative Principle. Neolithic cultures of Europe and the Near East, described in Chapter 2, celebrated the annual cycles of agricultural renewal by employing the myth of a young man and Goddess through the seasonal changes. This youth, initiated as a king or God, wooing the maiden Goddess in springtime, uniting with her in a Sacred Marriage in summer festivities, dies a sacrificial death in the fall. His death is not seen as a tragedy, but rather as a privilege necessary for springtime renewal. These myths anticipate the New Trinity through allegory.

Heide Göttner-Abendroth, in the English translation of her book, *The Goddess and Her Heroes* (1995), further traces the parallels of this myth and its variations through the millennia and across cultures beyond Europe, including Egypt, Persia, and India. The Goddess, herself, is successively transformed through seasonal changes, typically from the maiden Goddess of heaven, to a mature woman who is mistress of land and sea, and finally to a crone as Goddess of the underworld. In these roles, it is She who gives, then takes away, all things material. It is in the underworld—the unseen womb of gestation— where the fall seeds lie dormant to become the new life of springtime, completing the cycle of renewal.

Whereas the immortal Generative Principle allegorically lives through complete annual cycles continually transforming like phases of the moon, the masculine God is finite and mortal; he lives, dies, and then reappears in a new form. The masculine God is analogous to each of us as we live the finite cycle of our human life. Yet, there is another interpretation of this allegory that is very relevant to us as conscious beings. Each instant, our thoughts *die* in awareness as they are released into subconscious mind where they lie within the Generative Principle. Received by the Generative Principle, they are incubated and configured through Her formative powers into experience. Out of the privilege of conscious freedom, but also out of necessity for efficacious think- ing, we serve as the masculine God and continually fertilize the cosmic egg of creation. This myth of perpetual return is thus appli- cable to conscious life, as well as our human existence.

Göttner-Abendroth relates the seasons of spring, summer, and fall to the waxing, full, and waning phases of the moon (1995, 10-11). The silent dormancy of winter can then be related to the dark moon, which is analogous to subconsciousness within the creative process. The period following death, as described by Baring and Cashford, is likened unto the dark phase: "With death they would have felt that they were taken back into the dark womb of the Mother and believed that they would be reborn like the moon" (1992, 19).

Underlying the Sacred Marriage of the Neolithic period was the enduring Goddess encountered in the Paleolithic. Paleontologist Stephen Jay Gould commented upon the remarkable 32,000 BC wall art of the Chauvet Cave of France: "These paintings speak so powerfully to us because we know the people who did them; they are us" (1996, 73). Gould's theory is that evolutionary changes do not occur automatically in a linear progression, but happen in a step-wise fashion, only as required by external conditions. The Chauvet Cave contained remarkable art, continually practiced with little change during the next twenty millennia. It included symbols of the Goddess throughout this period, and apparently fulfilled societal needs for religious expression. Since the mastery of cave art was already well accomplished at the time of the Chauvet paintings, it must have existed much earlier, as well.

A great change requiring adaptation of human lifestyle occurred at the end of the ice age when glaciers retreated, effecting profound changes in the continental environment. Some animal herds moved northward, while others became extinct (Lister and Bahn, 1994, 119-137). These environmental alterations provided the opportunity and necessity for developing agricultural practices and domestication of animals that replaced, to a large extent, the

hunting of game animals. These changes did not require any evolutionary variation of the human species, but rather only behavioral
modifications. The formation of permanent settlements and atten-
dance to annual planting and harvesting cycles promoted additional mythical imagery, which eventually included the Sacred
Marriage. The older Goddess imagery was not replaced. Instead, it
was extended—with Her functions further differentiated, refined,
and embroidered into myths with allegorical meaning that corresponded to the increasing sophistication of society.

The tenure of the Goddess, from the Paleolithic, through the
Neolithic, and into and beyond the Bronze Age, spanned thirty
millennia. Thus, She is distinguished as the oldest archetypical representation. Proven through time to be fundamental, meaningful,
and important to the human psyche, She is appropriate to reestab-
lish into our mythical repertoire today. As Jung stated: "A symbol
is the best possible expression for an unconscious content whose
nature can only be guessed, because it is still unknown" (Jung,
1959, 6). The Goddess began as an archetype from the subconscious, as evidenced from the fact that She was represented symbolically, rather than pictorially like animal life. This practice is
apparent in the earliest archaeological knowledge of the European
continent, with a specific example being a simple vulva in the
Chauvet Cave (Chauvet, Deschamps, and Hillaire, 1996, 110).

The Goddess myths lived beyond the Neolithic through modified form into the present. Yet, it is the earlier versions, free from
later religious trappings, which reveal the intuitive human psyche,
and offer the closest concept to the meaning considered here. As
described in Chapter 2, this former notion of the Goddess
occurred prior to the emergence of the mythical Solar God manifesting in society by the male dominator. It was later, upon losing
perspective of the Goddess and misunderstanding Her products,
that Her antithesis was envisioned in the form of a male God,

delivering painful experiences out of judgmental anger. *Sin* was a concept advanced while pondering what could anger such a God, with forms of appeasement developed in attempts to satisfy Him. The appreciative celebration for harvest involved a petitioning sacrifice to this male God. The earlier Goddess was immanent in affairs of daily life, whereas the new Solar God was remote, invisibly residing in the sky until He eventually became abstract.

Communing With the Generative Principle

Carvings of the Goddess in stone, ivory, or bone are seen by archaeologists to be objects of veneration. Yet, functions of the Generative Principle operate within our lives whether acknowledged and venerated or not. However, there is value in acknowledging the Goddess, Soul, or the Feminine Generative Principle, and intimately knowing her in a personal manner, for such action facilitates recognizing the Divine Child in individual experience. This is especially so as it is important for us to acknowledge a power beyond ourselves in the providing of beneficent manifestations. Otherwise, we tend to falsely rely upon an inflated vision of our Human Selves, diminishing the spiritual perspective.

The Generative Principle is directly receptive to each person's thoughts and emotions, specifically incorporating them as kernels of belief in the universal womb of subconsciousness. The Generative Principle personalizes human experiences appropriate for each person, but She is *impersonal* in the particular form of Her response; that is, experiences are designed not to please or anger you, not to reward or punish you, but to represent the beliefs you have deposited with Her. She is non-judgmental in these presentations for She is not evaluating you or your actions, but only demonstrating your own evaluations. The Generative Principle, alone, determines Her manifestations through an intelligent ordering of natural processes and coordination of universal powers. An intelligent creative power, acting impartially upon *only* your beliefs within subconsciousness, must reasonably provide a cosmic justice. Consequently, it follows that the resulting experiences are *perfectly appropriate* for us.

From our limited human perspective, we judge these perfectly appropriate experiences. We decide, in relative terms, whether they appear either *good* or *bad*, whether they appear *associated with us* or *separated from us*, and whether we *accept* them or *deny* their reality, as outlined in Chapter 4. We stand alone before our experience in making these existential decisions, without knowing the content of our own subconscious and lacking the cosmic perspective of the Generative Principle. We rely only upon our subjective references of the moment, utilizing recalled values, and working toward our expectations of what we think should occur.

These judgmental evaluations form the basis for subsequent beliefs that we return to the Generative Principle in a continuous cycle. In order for us to change beliefs and consequential experiences—to step off the cycles of our self-constructed Karmic wheel—it is necessary to develop a new reference from which to judge each experience. Realization of a spiritual identity, separate from the human Ego, establishes such a reference. Experiences, both mental and physical, based upon this spiritual identity are more enjoyable and satisfying, and may be mythically personified as the Divine Child, the offspring of union with Spiritual Self and the Generative Principle.

As stated earlier, the meaning of the word *soul* has been inconsistent throughout the history of literature. James Hillman states that when we say, "soul is," that "we act out equally in the flight upward into the abstractions of metaphysics, higher philosophies, theologies, and even mysticism" (1992, 137). Indeed, it is a purpose of this book to provide a metaphysical basis for personal spirituality by drawing from the mythology and mysticism of past millennia. The intermediary between volitional conscious action and resulting experience deserves a name, and like the Generative Principle, *Soul* is an alternative candidate. Dynamically transforming beliefs into experiences, She is as much a verb as a noun, *a process of creation*.

The Vantage of Spirituality

Your spiritual identity, characterized in Chapter 4 and expanded upon in Chapter 7, is composed of freedom of thought in both awareness and decision. In spirit, it has inherent goodness, connectivity, equality with others, and existence in the *eternal now*, with unending creativity of conscious expression. This identity is not mysterious and not arrived at by esoteric means. Rather, it is the basic nature of your conscious mind. Your own physical body and the world around you provide a confusing veil, an apparent material reality that obscures this conscious reality.

Your human, material existence, involving a creature of time and space, stands in contrast to your conscious being. As a human, there are obstacles to freedom in terms of limitation, inadequacy, deficiency, inability, physical blockages, and bounds within time and space. The *perfectly appropriate experience* is subject to standards of material satisfaction, such as pleasure or pain, and with human judgment assigning quality in gradations of good to bad. Present conditions also are evaluated by their envisioned significance relative to the past or future. Seldom is the current moment considered alone without concern about possibilities of the future.

We encounter parades of people whom we love, admire, desire, fear, hate, or with whom we find offense. They come and go; we see them from afar, encounter them, and then they depart. Some we imagine but never meet, and some we meet and then forget. These encounters are projections from our sub-conscious mind, often beyond our control. Personal involve-ment by human standards involves temporal associations and rel-ative goodness—as distinct from the spiritual linkage of uncon-ditioned unification characterized by inherent goodness; a rela-tionship that may be called *spiritual love*.

The human identity involves a timeline beginning with birth, proceeding through childhood, maturity, into a period of physical decline, and ultimately the death of the body. During this period are cycles based upon physical attachments, such as achievement and failure, acquiring and losing possessions, and growing up then growing old. Always there is a perspective of time, although our consciousness identifying with this chronicle lives in the eternal moment.

The usual conditioning in our society associates primary identification with the human body and its environment. Therefore, many incorrectly believe that consciousness has no separate identity of its own, but is merely a consequence of the physical brain and nervous system, with personal identity being a composite of physical components with associated mental activities. We need to relate to both the physical and mental, but also make a distinction between the two. The physical body's network of neurological elements reflects an identity parallel to consciousness, with these two being *complementary* and *synchro-nized* through the Generative Principle as an intermediary con-stituting the third element of the New Trinity.

This choice regarding personal identity is so important that it is considered in this book as one of the *fundamental decisions* of conscious awareness. This judgment of personal association is pictured graphically within the States of Conscious Evaluation from Chapter 4 onward. Through subsequent chapters, we saw how all judgments of evaluation can be related to the coordinates which define the four states—where each event within awareness is evaluated in terms of being good or bad, according to its relationship to us.

This deductive reduction of all evaluation judgments is graphically portrayed within the States of Conscious Evaluation, illustrating how the varieties of everyday determinations are expressed as fundamental decisions. This approach provides an efficient and concise perspective of decisions made within the mind, and is valuable in understanding communications with the Generative Principle. It is important to comprehend the three states of consciousness outside of the Spiritual Self, so that differences in judgment represented within these three states can be reversed, if so desired.

The States of Conscious Evaluation are expanded in Chapter 6 to include the realm of emotion. Each familiar emotion is shown to have direct correspondence with evaluations in thought. Thus, awareness of emotion aids in understanding what type of cognitive judgments underlies each experience. Emotions occur in all communication with the Generative Principle, both in experiences given by Her and through our own conscious response. In the prior case, emotions occur immediately, with psychic experience providing an indicator of thoughts composing prior beliefs. Note that the psychic experience is *personalized* for each physical manifestation and, therefore, may not be the same for other persons. The significance of experience can thus be understood through accompanying emotions arriving in response to the event.

Chapters 8 and 9 amplify those thoughts and emotions particular to evaluations of the Human Self, the self-composed identity relative to the material world. All human experience is marked with uncertainty of what will next occur, for it is the Generative Principle, rather than we, that is in control of external events. Degrees of anxiety resulting from this uncertainty are inherent to human dependency upon material events.

The fundamental judgment of quality is subjectively applied to both consciousness and to physical experiences. Even though goodness is the reality of consciousness, we may judge otherwise through freedom or misconception. Our Spiritual Self and its fundamental nature can then be obscured by judgments of self-depreciation, possibly leading to conditions of depression with shadings of hopelessness, shame, despair, or anguish, as described in Chapter 10.

While it is helpful to rationally understand judgments behind various states of consciousness and realize how to return to a spiritual orientation, the process requires effort. Knowledge of one's spiritual identity is an important step toward enlightenment, but as Stephen Levine suggested, enlightenment does not improve character; rather, enlightenment is simply a type of awareness. Therefore, the enlightened awareness of your Spiritual Self, alone, does not in any way insure that the character of your human personality shall express the divine. Your intentions and actions, both conscious and physical, are required to achieve this. Your own divine nature will express through experiences of fulfillment, joy, freedom, and peace as you integrate a spiritual identity into your system of beliefs. This incorporation of the spiritual into self-identity is assisted by techniques of meditation, as examined in Chapters 11 and 12.

The Spiritual Self is immersed within a world of materiality, with the human persona worn by consciousness like a costume. The physical world as provided by the Generative Principle, with all its entailing pain and pleasure, is appropriate for each moment, providing media for expression, demonstration, and opportunity. Through mindfulness and reflection, we can see a distinction between the realms of cause and effect. We realize that we are not victims of random circumstances, or of a judgmental, seemingly unjust, autocratic supreme being. Instead, we have inherent worth with freedom to exercise a conscious efficacy, which empowered through the Generative Principle, creates a better demonstration of goodness.

Recognizing and affirming spiritual identity facilitates its manifestation by the Generative Principle. Chapter 13 describes affirmative meditation as a deliberate mental action effective in this endeavor. This special type of meditation is directly applied to realizing qualities of spiritual nature, embracing them within personal identity, and affirming their truth well beyond abstract knowledge. Affirmative meditation employs all three fundamental judgments identified in Chapter 3, i.e., quality, association, and acceptance. Whereas the first two components are used in self-evaluation and may be intellectually acknowledged, acceptance is a mental *action of admission* necessary for fruition. This mental act of allowance implements the verbal statement: *So it is*, and *so it shall be.*

We do not think a lot about our action of acceptance, yet it is important that we complete this process in order to insure that our thoughts become incorporated into beliefs. Only by this means do we culminate the Sacred Marriage with the Generative Principle. It is helpful to be aware of the subtle decision of acceptance during the practice of affirmative meditation, otherwise we may disown our goodness of being.

The Divine Child Incarnate

The Divine Child occurs in consciousness as one's inherent spiritual nature is realized and embraced, thus projecting peace, a sense of well-being, and joy of life. It entails connectivity with other beings, including a bond of love and empathy. This realization leads to a conscious self-esteem that embraces the Spiritual Self and supplements human self-esteem. Realistic human self-esteem, balanced by humility, complements you as a worthy and capable person. If such human self-esteem is not supported by spiritual awareness, then it has no grounding and eventually will crumble. Whereas Spiritual self-esteem leads to right action and good works, human self-esteem may have an egocentric directive that eventually will be disrupted through material cycles of building up and tearing down.

With its confirming manifestations contributing to a sense of expression and fulfillment, the physical body holds a complementary position to the spiritual being. As Hegel observed: "Freedom in thought has only *pure thought* as its truth, a truth lacking the fullness of life." And, he further added: "The True and the Good shall consist in reasonableness. But this self-identity of pure thought is again only the pure form in which nothing is determined [that is, without manifestation]. The True and the Good, wisdom and virtue, the general terms beyond which Stoicism cannot get, are therefore in a general way no doubt uplifting, but since they cannot produce any expansion of content [no demonstration, either material or emotional], they soon become tedious," (1977, 122).

Affirmative meditation is uplifting and, invoking an emotional response, it leads to peace and well-being. But it cannot through itself, alone, bring about the specific content of human experience. Consciousness initiates the generative process, but requires the Sacred Marriage with the Generative Principle to expand upon the particularities of goodness through Her determination. Otherwise, as Hegel expressed, we might eventually find purely mental processes to be tedious. In other words, masculine consciousness must embrace and *demonstrate* its own fundamental nature to facilitate the Divine Marriage with the feminine Generative Principle and, thus, produce the Divine Child.

The incarnation of the Divine Child is an archetypal phenomenon, where the transcendent becomes immanent and the Word becomes flesh. Some theologians view Christ, "God born in human form," as a one-time, historical event. Alternatively, however, this account provides a powerful archetypical allegory relative to personal spirituality, where there is the potential for a similar incarnation to occur in each individual consciousness, that is, a *Christ consciousness*. It is often helpful to view our religious myths in the manner of the ancients. For example, Mircea Eliade in *The Myth of Eternal Return* describes the *ontological conception*: "An object or act becomes real only insofar as it imitates or repeats an archetype. Thus, reality is acquired solely through repetition or participation; everything which lacks an exemplary model is 'meaningless,' i.e., it lacks reality" (Eliade, 1971, 34). In this perspective, to give human expression to the Divine Child is to bring into your life an incarnation of the archetype represented by, for example, the Christ, Krishna, or Buddha.

Heinrich Zimmer, relating the Hindu myth of Krishna as the progeny of the Supreme God Vishnu and a human mother, stated: "For the human avatar [Krishna] is a blending of opposites. Such a blending also, are we ourselves, though unaware of our twofold nature: we are at once the unlimited, unconditioned, divine Self, and the surrounding attributes of personality-experience and ego-consciousness" (Zimmer, 1992, 89).

This dual perspective—the simultaneous viewing of the outer physical world along with the realization of your conscious, spiritual being—is necessary for a truly objective evaluation of your choices. It is also necessary for selected actions leading to a physical incarnation of the Divine Child, the phenomenal manifestation of spiritual nature as expressed through your own unique human experience. Do not be concerned with another's expectations of the divine, for a divine manifestation could not be other than incomparable, expressing infinite creativity. It is sufficient to just be your own magnificent self.

Your expectations of how the Divine Child should appear can be a hindrance, as they are attachments to preconceived worldly imagery. For some people, Mother Teresa and Mahatma Gandhi might personify ideal Divine Children, yet their demonstrations were peculiar to their situation and culture. Their lives may be inspiring, but they may not represent appropriate models for your circumstances. Many Divine Children lead quiet, unassuming lives that reflect love and peace through seemingly ordinary experiences. You have your own unique conditions on this earth; therefore, there is no exact precedent to determine your response.

Incarnation of the Divine Child is, in a sense, an imitation of one of the many masters, yet accomplished in the unique style of your own character, like a musician providing a variation on a theme. Identical imitation becomes unnecessary by realizing the creative potential made possible through the union of individual spirit and the Generative Principle. Furthermore, your greatest reward is inward, not outward; it is not necessary that you attain great recognition or conform to preconceived standards. Even the virtues of morality and ethics are but reflections of inner values that express your personal integrity and the many forms of love. It is sufficient that you actualize your spiritual nature during daily affairs in your own unique manner.

Do not expect a permanent transformation of experience or character, but rather accept the good occasions as they occur. Be tolerant with yourself, for you are still human and likely have many undesirable situations yet to manifest during your earthly experience. You can always look within and say, *Life is good!* But, more and more frequently may you say, *I really feel good about my existence today!* When you do recognize the Divine Child as an aspect of yourself, appreciate and nurture its presence and bid it to soon return. Such a reception will increase the frequency of its appearance.

The transformation of this world into a more joyful, peaceful, and caring place will take time. But, it can only be accomplished as individuals realize their spiritual identities. Discovering one's spiritual nature requires self-conscious awareness. Yet, paradoxically, to be alive and effective as a human requires one to put aside self-consciousness for the moment and to live with awareness in the world of now. Find your personal passions and pursue them with vibrancy, excitement, and a sense of adventure—fearlessly acting beyond the expectations of others and above the norm. Paint your life as a work of art with the pallet from the Generative Principle, drawing from Her infinite supply. As She is your ground of being, view your expressions as Her own as well, as though you are both Her eyes and hands.

Questions for Discussion

(1) How does the ancient myth of the male God, united with the Goddess, dying, and reborn, allegorically relate to you as both a human and conscious being?

(2) In what way is the Generative Principle impersonal and non-judgmental in Her response to you?

(3) Why are human experiences produced by the Generative Principle termed as *perfectly appropriate* if they are sometimes painful as well as pleasant?

(4) How can you bring an incarnation of the mythical Divine Child into your life for improved experience?

(5) Why might the occurrence of the Divine Child be beyond worldly expectations?

Developing a spiritual paradigm for the new
millennium begins with your decision to
take action in this eternal now.

REFERENCES AND RESOURCES

Armstrong, A. H., 1981. *An Introduction to Ancient Philosophy.* Rowman & Littlefield Publishers, Inc.

Armstrong, Karen. 1994. *A History of God.* New York: Ballentine Books.

Baring, Ann, and Cashford, Jules. 1992. *The Myth of the Goddess.* London: Penguin Books.

Blyth, R. H. 1942. *Zen in English Literature and Oriental Classics.* Tokyo: The Hokuseidao Press.

Bohm, David. 1980. *Wellness and the Implicate Order.* London and New York: Routledge & Kegan Paul.

Bolen, Jean Shenoda. 1989. *Gods in Everyman.* San Francisco: Harper & Row, Publishers.

Bradshaw, John. 1988. *Healing the Shame that Binds You.* Dearfield Beach: Health Communications, Inc.

Branden, Nathaniel. 1971. *The Psychology of Self-Esteem.* New York: Bantam Books, Inc.

Buber, Martin. 1987. *I and Thou.* New York: Collier Books.

Campbell, Joseph. 1969. *The Masks of God: Primitive Mythology.* New York: Penguin Books.
——. 1972. *The Hero with a Thousand Faces.* Princeton: Princeton University Press.

——. 1988. *Historical Atlas of World Mythology, Vol. I: The Way of Animal Powers*. New York, Harper & Row.

——. 1988. *The Inner Reaches of Outer Space: Metaphor as Myth and as Religion*. New York: Harper & Row, Perennial Library.

Cermak, Timmen L. 1986. *Diagnosing and Treating Co-dependency*. Minneapolis: Johnson Institute Books.

Chalmers, David J. 1996 *The Conscious Mind: In Search of a Fundamental Theory*. New York: Oxford University Press.

Chauvet, Jean-Marie, Eliette Brunel Deschamps, and Christian Hillaire. 1996. *Dawn of Art: The Chauvet Cave*. New York: Harry N. Abrams, Inc.

Damasio, Antonio. 1999. *The Feeling of What Happens: Body and Emotion in the Making of Consciousness*. San Diego: Harcourt, Inc.

Dillaway, Newton. 1990. *The Gospel of Emerson*. Unity Village: Unity Books.

Dossey, Larry. 1993. *Healing Words*. San Francisco: HarperCollins Publishers.

Emerson, Ralph Waldo. 1926. *Essays by Ralph Waldo Emerson*. New York: Harper & Row, Publishers.

Flach, Frederic F. 1974. *The Secret Strength of Depression*. Philadelphia and New York: J. P. Lippincott Company.

Frazier, Sir James George. 1963. *The Golden Bough*. New York: Macmillan Publishing Company.

Fromm, Erich. 1956. *The Art of Loving.* New York: Harper and Row, Publishers.

Gardner, Howard. 1983. *Frames of Mind: The Theory of Multiple Intelligences.* New York: Basic Books.

Gimbutas, Marija. 1989. *The Language of the Goddess.* New York: HarperCollins Publishers.

Goldman, Daniel. 1995. *Emotional Intelligence.* New York: Bantam Books.

Goldstein, Joseph, and Jack Kornfield. 1987. *Seeking the Heart of Wisdom.* Boston: Shambhala Publications, Inc.

Göttner-Abendroth, Heide. 1995. *The Goddess and Her Heros.* Stow: Anthony Publishing Company.

Gould, Stephen Jay. 1996. "Up Against a Wall." *Natural History* 105 (7).

Grigg, Ray. 1994. *The Tao of Zen.* Boston: Charles E. Tuttle Co., Inc.

Hawkes, Jacquetta. 1993. *The Atlas of Early Man.* New York: St. Martin's Press, Inc.

Hegel, G. W. F. 1977. *Phenomenology of Spirit.* Oxford: Oxford University Press.

Hess, Hermann. 2000. *Siddhartha*. Boston: Shambhala Publications, Inc.

Hillman, James. 1960. *Emotion*. Evanston: Northwest University Press.
———. 1992. *Re-Visioning Psychology*. New York: HarperCollins Publishers.
———. 1996. *The Soul's Code*. New York: Random House.

Jung, C. G.1959. *Archetypes and the Collective Unconscious*. Princeton: Princeton University Press.
———. 1964. *Man and His Symbols*. New York: Doubleday & Company.
———. 1973. *Answer to Job*. Princeton: Princeton University Press.

Kauffman, Stuart A. 2008. *Reinventing the Sacred: A New View of Science, Reason and Religion*. New York: Basic Books.

Kaufmann, Walter. 1956. *Nietzsche: Philosopher, Psychologists, Antichrist*. New York: Meridian Books.

Kierkegaard, Søren. 1980. *The Concept of Anxiety*. Princeton: Princeton University Press.

Levine, Stephen. 1987. *Healing into Life and Death*. New York: Anchor Books.
———. 1991. *Guided Meditations, Explorations, and Healings*. New York: Anchor Books.

Lister, Adrian and Paul Bahn. 1994. *Mammoths*. New York: Macmillian, Inc.

May, Rollo. 1977. *The Meaning of Anxiety*. New York: W. W. Norton & Company, Inc.

Mellody, Pia. 1989. *Facing Codependency*. San Francisco: Harper & Row, Publishers.

Moran, Dermot. 2000. *Introduction to Phenomenology*. London and New York: Routledge.

Niebuhr, Reinhold. 1964. *The Nature and Destiny of Man*. New York: Charles Scribner's Sons.

Neumann, Erich. 1972. *The Great Mother*. Princeton: Princeton University Press.
——. 1995. *The Origins and History of Consciousness*. Princeton: Princeton University Press.

Ornstein, Robert. 1986. *The Psychology of Consciousness*. New York: Penguin Books.

Peck, M. Scott. 1979. *The Road Less Traveled*. New York: Simon & Schuster.

Perls, Frederick S. 1971. *Gestalt Therapy Verbatim*. New York: Bantam Books, Inc.
——. 1976. *The Gestalt Approach & Eye Witness to Therapy*. New York: Bantam Books, Inc.

Plutchik, Robert. 1991. *The Emotions*. Lanham: University Press of America, Inc.

Sardello, Robert. 1992. *Facing the World with Soul*. Hudson: Lindisfarne Press.

Sartre, Jean-Paul. 1956. *Being and Nothingness*. New York: Philosophical Library.
———. 1993. *The Emotions*. Secaucus: Carol Publishing.

Siegel, Daniel J. 2007. *The Mindful Brain, Reflection and Attunement in the Cultivation of Well-Being*. New York: W. W. Norton & Company.

Solomon, Robert C. 1980. Emotions and Choice. In *Explaining Emotions*. ed. Amelie Oksenberg Rorty. Berkeley: University of California Press.
———. 2007. *True To Our Feelings: What Emotions are Really Telling Us*. New York: Oxford University Press.

Spinoza, Benedict. 1955. *On the Improvement of the Understanding, The Ethics, Correspondence*. New York: Dover Publications, Inc.

Suzuki, Shunryu. 1973. *Zen Mind, Beginner's Mind*. New York: Weatherhill, Inc.

Tillich, Paul. 1963. *The Eternal Now*. New York: Charles Scribner's Sons.

Wilhelm, Richard. 1962. *The Secret of the Golden Flower*. San Diego: Harcourt Brace Jovanovich, Publishers. Commentary by C. G. Jung, originally delivered as a memorial address for R. Wilhelm in Munich, 1930.

Zimmer, Heinrich. 1969. *Philosophies of India*. ed. Joseph Campbell. Princeton: Princeton University Press.
——. 1992. *Myths and Symbols in Indian Art and Civilization*. ed. Joseph Campbell. Princeton: Princeton University Press, Mythos edition.

Jack Burch

Jack J. Burch set aside an early attraction to philosophy and psychology and pursued his other interest of engineering. He received Bachelor and Master of Science Degrees in Electrical Engineering at Southern Methodist University, with additional graduate studies in mathematics. Jack followed a career at Texas Instruments in Dallas that included ten years of research in electro-optics.

Leaving the corporate world, Jack with his wife Lynda undertook a succession of entrepreneurial ventures, resulting in a series of galleries in the Southwest featuring Mother Nature's art, each called the Mineral & Fossil Gallery. After divesting from this business, Jack now spends his time writing and developing programs for personal spirituality in the local community, while practicing his philosophy.

Throughout his life, Jack engaged his continued interest in metaphysical philosophy, especially in the ontology of spiritual identity. He studied Religious Science, and served as a licensed practitioner for five years teaching classes. Leaving that movement, Jack developed his ideas of metaphysics along with its related psychology. He formulated a model for spiritual identity existing within each conscious mind, and developed mindfulness practices leading to enhanced life experiences, with this work resulting in The New Trinity.

Jack and his wife live in Albuquerque, and follow their interests in yoga, the arts, travel, food, and wine. Jack swims and frequently hikes in the New Mexico mountains.